Exploring Attributes

Maria Marolda

Exploring Attributes

Activities for the 32-block set and the 60-block set

Dale Seymour Publications

Dedicated to the set of people
who have been, are, and
always will be very special to me:
Tony, Matt, and Ria

Project Editor: Joan Gideon
Cover Design: Rachel Gage
Design: Michelle Taverniti
Production Coordinators: Karen Edmonds/Barbara Atmore

ISBN 0-86651-672-7
Printed in the United States of America
    9 10   06 05 04

1-800-321-3106
www.pearsonlearning.com

Contents

Introduction

Attribute materials are a rich mathematical resource. As students look for similarities and differences or analyze and complete attribute-block patterns, they build their understanding of relationships. As they sort the materials into sets and subsets, use Venn diagrams, and learn the mathematical language of logical connectives *(and, or, not)*, students build their logical thinking skills. After they become familiar with these ideas, students can begin using the same techniques to analyze data and develop problem-solving strategies.

Exploring Attributes offers activities you can use to make the most of attribute materials in your classroom. The simpler activities (Sections 1, 2, and 3) are appropriate for primary students, but are not too simplistic for older children. Some of the activities involving more sophisticated thinking strategies (Sections 3, 4, and 5) are challenging for students in grades 4–8; primary students can also complete many of these activities.

The *Curriculum and Evaluation Standards for School Mathematics*, prepared by the National Council of Teachers of Mathematics, states that good mathematics instruction includes problem solving, communication, reasoning, and patterns and relationships. Students experience all of these as they use the activities from *Exploring Attributes*.

Attribute Materials

To use these activities, you will need sets of attribute blocks. These are commercially available or can be made from the blackline masters on page ix and xi. The original "Attribute Blocks" created by the Elementary Science Study (ESS) consisted of 32 wooden blocks in four geometric shapes (square, triangle, diamond, circle), four colors (red, blue, yellow, green), and two sizes (large, small). Over the years, a variety of other attribute blocks have emerged, including the 60-piece Invicta Desk Top Attributes in five shapes (square, rectangle, triangle, hexagon, circle), three colors (red, blue, yellow), two sizes (large, small), and two thicknesses (thick, thin).

The activities in this book are compatible with these two attribute block sets and are also adaptable to individually created attribute materials. Attribute materials need not be limited to physical blocks of geometric shapes, but can be any set of elements with varying characteristics. For example, the original ESS materials included a set called People Pieces, having the attributes male or female, fat or thin, tall or short, and wearing red or blue clothing. Teachers and children can create their own unique sets of attribute materials—for example, dogs or vehicles with different attributes—and use them for activities similar to those suggested for geometric attribute blocks. Section 6 contains two attribute sets like those students can make.

Logical Problem Solving

Once students are comfortable with the concepts and strategies developed using attribute blocks, the same ideas are extended to more general problem-solving situations. Using first data they collect about themselves and through other surveys, students learn how to organize and analyze information in Venn diagrams. These activities help students link what they have learned using attribute materials to their work with story problems, making them seem more familiar and relevant.

Since logical problem solving is ideally suited to cooperative group work, the student pages in Section 5 are designed to be used by groups of four students. Individual students can also solve the problems given all four pieces of information.

Using the Activities

The activities in *Exploring Attributes* are grouped in six sections:

1. Getting Acquainted
2. Making Patterns
3. Difference Activities
4. Loop Activities
5. Problem Solving
6. Feature Creatures and Hot-Air Balloons

Each section contains several types of activity sheets. Teaching notes for each type are given on a page preceding the activities. Use the activities that are suitable for your class starting with the sorting activities. Problems involving the not-sets are at the end of the section for each set of attribute blocks. They may be too difficult for some primary students and can be omitted by primary teachers. The Difference Activities may be difficult for students of any age—allow students to work at their own pace. Be sure that students thoroughly understand the **Difference Trains** before they attempt **Different in Both Directions**. The **Two-Set** and **Three-Set Problems** in Section 5 are intended for middle-school students or for gifted elementary students.

The *Exploring Attributes* activities are presented on reproducible sheets that can be used by individual students, by small cooperative groups, or in teacher-led instructional settings. Activities in the first four sections involve sets of attribute blocks. Those pages marked *32-block set* can be used with the 32-piece attribute block set, while those marked *60-block set* are for use with the 60-piece attribute block set. Pages marked *32- or 60-block set* may be used with either set. Some of the activity sheets have open-ended formats that students and teachers can use to design their own activities.

A simple code is used on the activity sheets to indicate specific blocks. Shapes are the square, triangle, circle, and diamond. A letter indicates color, and capitalization of the letter indicates a large block, while lowercase indicates a small block.

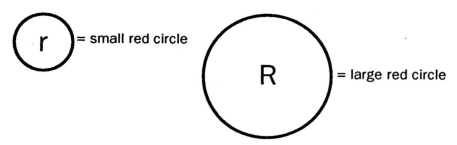

The code for the 32-piece attribute block set is maintained for the 60-piece attribute block set, the shapes hexagon and rectangle are added, and thickness is indicated with shading.

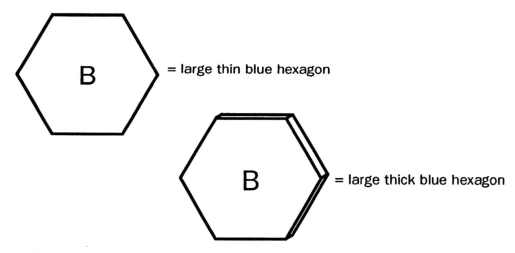

Students can complete some of the activities by placing blocks on the activity sheets or by drawing blocks on the sheets using the code. They can also reproduce a problem with the blocks before solving it.

When students are using the actual blocks to solve the problems, you will need to check responses as they complete each activity. Students might work in pairs and check each other's work. Sheets that are completed with attribute blocks may be used again and again. Promote flexible and creative thinking by asking, "Is there any other way of solving this challenge?" The ability to find multiple solutions is an important part of mathematical reasoning. If your students keep a math journal, ask them to write about the multiple solutions to some of the problems.

For activities using loops or Venn diagrams, tie yarn or string in large loops (as much as 18 inches in diameter) and spread them out on the work surface. For three-loop activities, rigid loops are preferable, since they make it easier to maintain the arrangement. Rigid loops can be made from wire coat hangers; plastic loops are available commercially.

The activities in this book should be extended to problems created by the students. Asking them to create their own problems will help all students thoroughly understand the concepts. Students can make copies of their problems for other students to solve. Students who keep a math notebook or journal can record the problems they write and put into words how they devised the problem and how they checked it to be sure it worked. Other good prompts for a math journal include, "How did you solve this problem?" and "How would you put into words the rule for this pattern you made?"

Using the Reproducible Attribute Materials

Immediately following this Introduction, you will find blackline masters you can copy to create paper sets of attribute shapes. For a complete 32-piece set, you will need four copies of page xi, preferably duplicated on a heavy card stock. The students then color the shapes on each sheet in a different color (red, green, blue, yellow) and cut them apart—either by cutting out the actual shapes, or by cutting on the straight lines to make sets of cards. For a 60-piece set, use page xiii and make three copies, to be colored in red, blue, and yellow. If your copy machine allows you to copy on colored construction paper, the coloring step can be skipped.

The label cards and difference cards on pages xii and xiv are useful for sorting and other attribute activities. Duplicate one label page for each complete set of attribute blocks in your classroom.

The blackline master on page 115 gives you another sets of attribute materials—the Feature Creatures. This clan of fanciful creatures, with varying facial and body features, may be used as an extension to the attribute blocks for many of the activities. The blackline masters on page 123 give yet another set of attribute materials—the Hot-Air Balloons. As students use three different color schemes to color the three patterns in three sizes, they create a colorful set of attribute materials that can be used with a wide variety of activities. The Feature Creatures and Hot-Air Balloons are introduced, with special activities, in Section 6.

Students will learn as they extend the ideas and formats of this book to creating their own sorting activities, patterns, or puzzles, and as they write about their thinking. *Exploring Attributes* is designed to build mathematical concepts and ideas by actively engaging students in their own learning and instilling in them a joy in the activity of logical problem solving.

32-Block Attribute Set

Make four copies—one each of red, blue, yellow, and green.

32-Block Attribute Set Label Cards

blue	red	yellow	green
△	◯	▢	◇
large	small	not large	not small
not blue	not red	not yellow	not green
⟁not	(not)	▢not	◇not

Difference Cards

1-difference	2-difference	3-difference

different in 1 way	different in 2 ways

different in 3 ways

60-Block Attribute Set

Make three copies—one each of red, blue, and yellow

60-Block Attribute Set Label Cards

red	blue	yellow	□
▭	△	⬡	○
large	small	thick	thin
not red	not blue	not yellow	□ not
▭ not	△ not	⬡ not	○ not
not large	not small	not thick	not thin

Difference Cards

1-difference	2-difference	3-difference

4-difference

different in 1 way	different in 2 ways

different in 3 ways	different in 4 ways

Sorting

Purpose

- To explore and become familiar with the attribute blocks.
- To classify attribute blocks into sets.
- To learn the coding system that identifies attribute blocks in this book.

Materials

✔ **Sorting** (page 3), used with 32- or 60-block set

Teaching Notes

Before distributing the activity sheet, let the students explore the attribute blocks in free play. All students need some sorting activities to become familiar with the blocks. Younger students should spend more time with informal sorting activities at the concrete level, while older students might spend less time with the actual blocks before starting the activity sheet.

After a period of free time with the blocks, ask the students to sort the blocks according to some systematic procedure. Some students may sort the blocks into groups according to an attribute, such as red blocks, while others might sort the blocks into some physical arrangement, such as a square array.

Sorting asks the students to focus on specific aspects of the set of attribute blocks. Each student or pair of students should be working with one set of blocks and an activity sheet.

Introduce the coding of the blocks used on the activity sheet. The letter of the alphabet indicates the color the block. Capital letters indicate large blocks, while lowercase letters indicate small blocks. For the 60-block set, shading will indicate thickness (not pictured on this page so the page can be used with both sets of blocks). Students can match the actual blocks to those pictured on the sheet. Students might color the pictured blocks to help acquaint them with the coding system.

Explain that the word *attribute* refers to the different characteristics they have observed in the blocks—shape, color, size, and thickness (for 60-block set) are all attributes of the blocks.

Extensions

Students might sort and classify other sets of objects, such as the Feature Creatures and Hot-Air Balloons (introduced in Section 6), or small items such as shells, leaves, buttons, beads, tiles, or coins. Discuss the different attributes of each set.

Sorting

Sort the blocks—put them into sets.

How many sets did you form? _____

Describe each set.

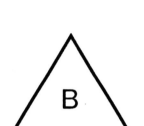

Sort the blocks in another way.

How many sets did you form? _____

Describe each set.

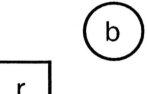

Find as many ways to sort the blocks as you can.

Describe each of these ways.

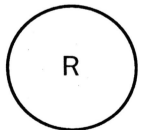

In the Loop

Purpose

- To introduce the loop as a mechanism for sorting specific sets.
- To introduce the label cards as a means of naming the set inside the loop.
- To introduce negative sets (not-sets) as well as positive ones (for intermediate and middle-school students).

Materials

✔ **In the Loop Activity A, B, C** (pages 5–7), used with 32- or 60-block set, label cards, and yarn loops (optional)

Teaching Notes

As the students use **In the Loop Activity A** and **B**, talk with them about what they put in the loop and about what is left outside the loop.

In the Loop Activity C can be used repeatedly with different label cards. For a group activity at the concrete level, you might hold up a label card, while the students place the proper blocks in the loop. For students working in pairs, one might turn over a label card, while the other sorts the blocks. The first student would then check the results.

Intermediate and middle-school students can be introduced to not-sets Using **In the Loop Activity C**. Because the not-sets tend to be larger than the positive sets, you might prefer to do this activity with large yarn loops.

For a pencil-and-paper activity, ask students to write the label on the sheet and draw (with appropriate coding) the blocks that belong in the loop. Or ask the students to write about the sorting activities.

Extensions

In the Loop—a game for two players (or two teams).

- Use **In the Loop Activity C** or a yarn loop. Shuffle the positive-set (no not-sets) label cards and scatter them face down in the center of the table.
- One player picks a label card, looks at it without showing the other player, and then places the card face down next to the loop.
- The second player chooses a block and asks, "Does this block belong in the loop?" The player then places the block inside or outside the loop, according to the first player's response. Note that students learn as much from a "no" response as a "yes."

The goal of the game is to determine what is on the label card by asking as few questions as possible. To make the game even more challenging, use label cards for the not-sets.

In the Loop

Place the blocks in the loop according to the label card.

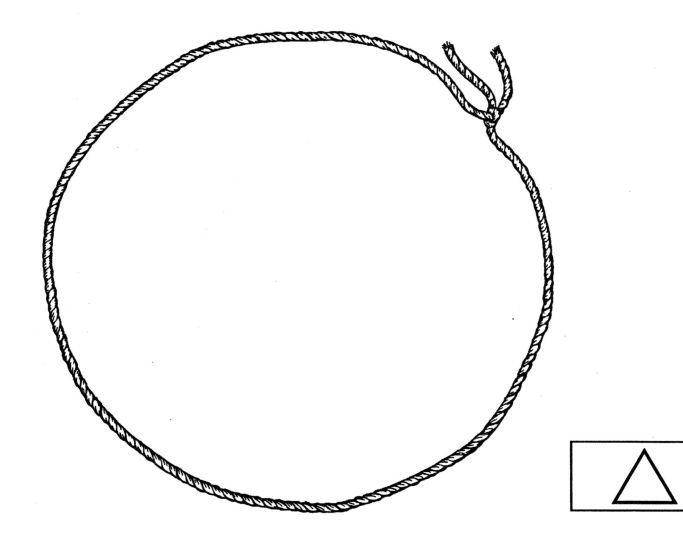

How many blocks are in the loop? _____

There are _____ blocks in the set of triangles.

How many blocks are outside the loop? _____

There are _____ blocks that are not triangles.

In the Loop

Activity B

Place the blocks in the loop according to the label card.

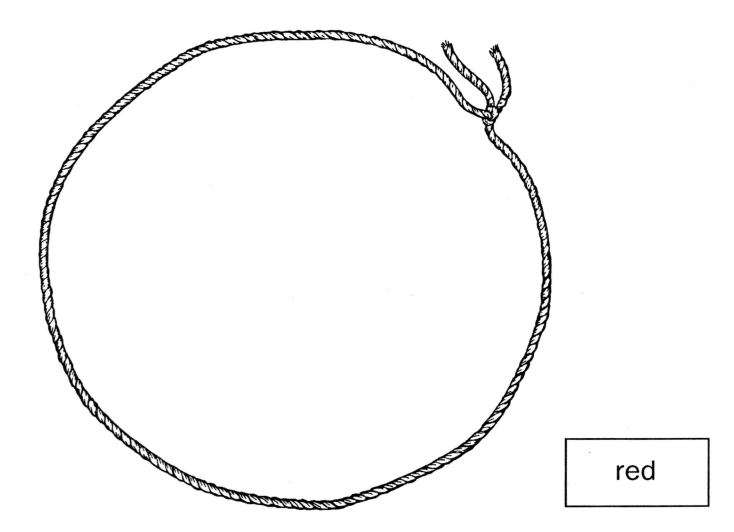

red

How many blocks are in the loop? _____

There are _____ blocks in the set of red blocks.

How many blocks are outside the loop? _____

There are _____ blocks that are not red.

(32- or 60-block set)

In the Loop

Activity C

Place the blocks in the loop according to the label card.

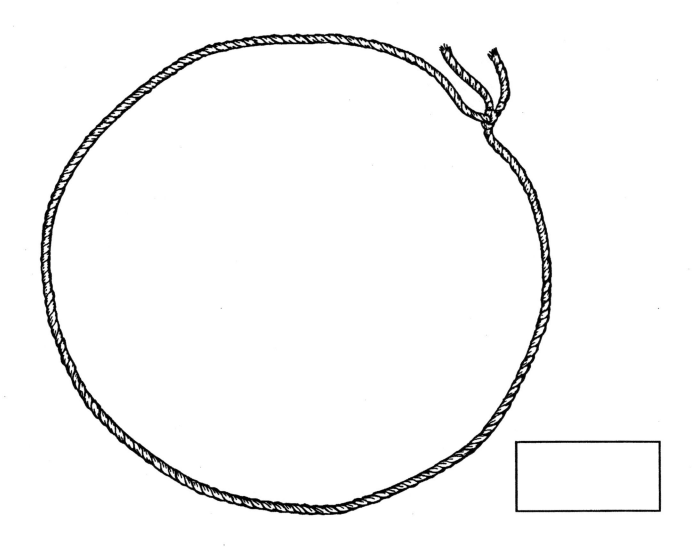

How many blocks are in the loop? _____

There are _____ blocks in the set of _____.

How many blocks are outside the loop? _____

There are _____ blocks that are not _____.

Name the Set

Purpose

- To name pictured sets according to their elements.

Materials

✔ **Name the Set Activity A, B, C, D** (pages 9–12), used with 32-block set and label cards

✔ **Name the Set Activity E, F, G, H, I** (pages 13–17), used with 60-block set and label cards

Teaching Notes

These activities develops "reverse processing," a strategy useful in general problem solving and critical thinking.

If students are having difficulty with this activity, let them use yarn loops and the actual blocks to recreate the set shown on the sheet. Seeing what is left outside the loop may help them identify the set involved.

Not-sets are pictured on **Name the Set Activity D** and **Activity I**.

Extensions

Concentration—a game for two players (or two teams).

Create a set of One-Loop cards that picture the ten or twelve positive subsets that can be described with a label card. Cut apart each activity sheet and mount on 5-by-7 index cards the individual loops that picture positive subsets. (Be sure the label boxes are left blank.) There are ten of these subsets for the 32-block set and twelve for the 60-block set.

- One player mixes the One-Loop cards and lays them face down in a rectangular array on the floor or a large table. The label cards are then mixed and placed in a rectangular array below the One-Loop cards.

- Players take turns turning over a One-Loop card and a label card. If the label card describes the set pictured on the One-Loop card, the player keeps those two cards and takes another turn. If the label card does not describe the set of blocks pictured, both cards are turned face down in their original positions.

- Play continues until all cards are used. The player with the most matches wins.

Name the Set

Activity A

Find the label card to describe the set of blocks in each loop.

1.

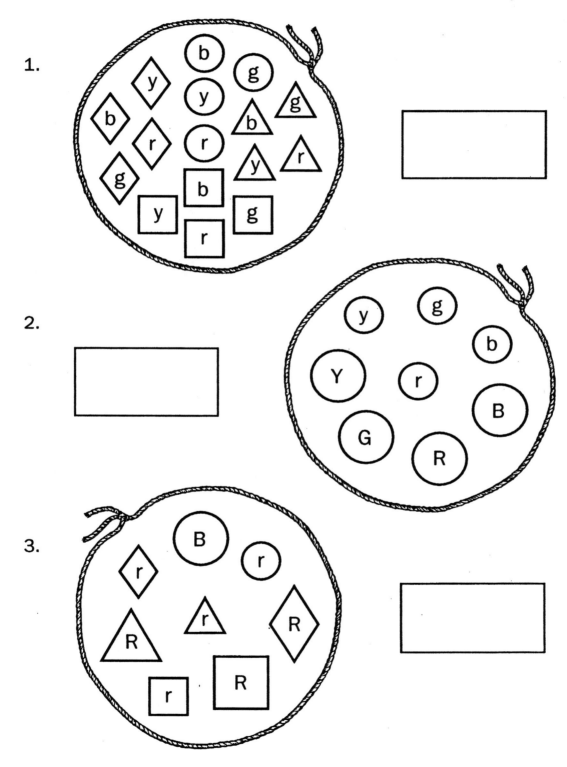

2.

3.

Name the Set

Find the label card to describe the set of blocks in each loop.

1.

2.

3.

(32-block set)

Name the Set

Activity C

Find the label card to describe the set of blocks in each loop.

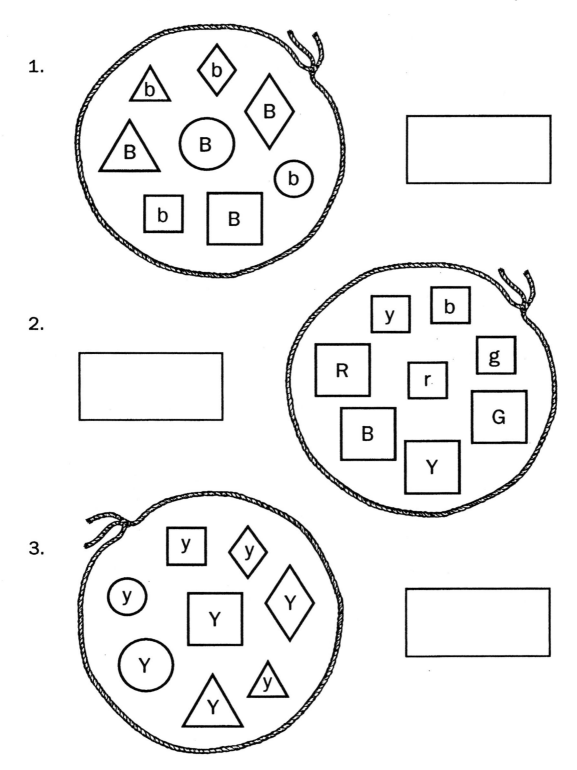

1.

2.

3.

Name the Set

Activity D

Find the label card to describe the set of blocks in each loop.

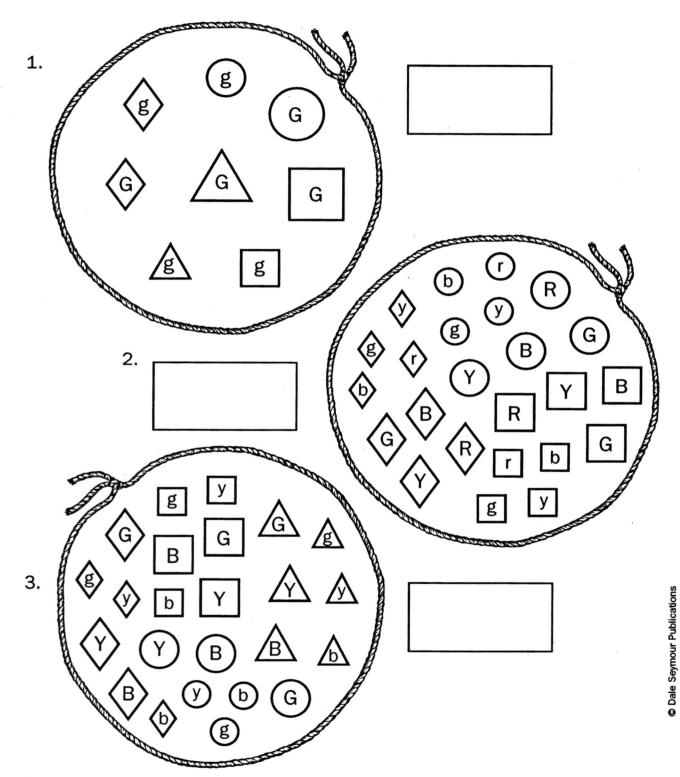

(32-block set)

Name the Set

Activity E

Find the label card to describe the set of blocks in each loop.

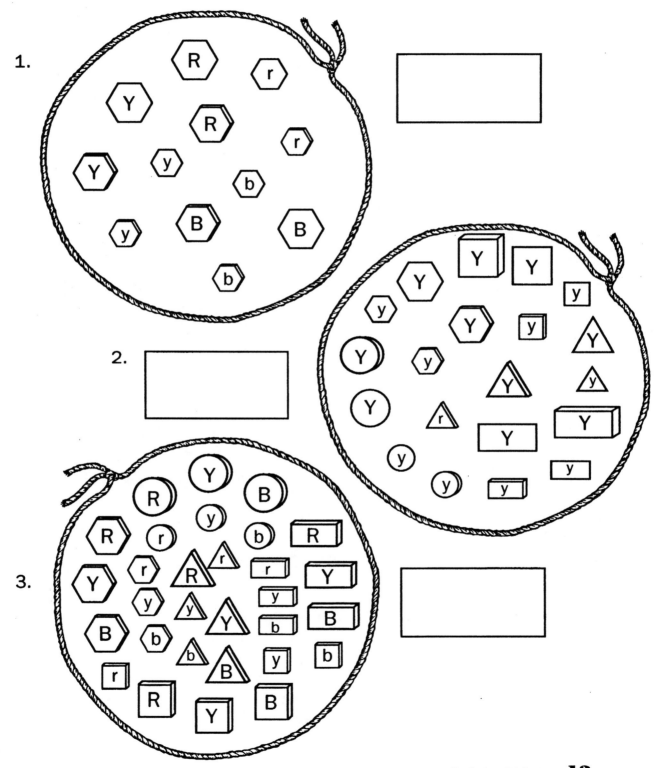

1.

2.

3.

Name the Set

Find the label card to describe the set of blocks in each loop.

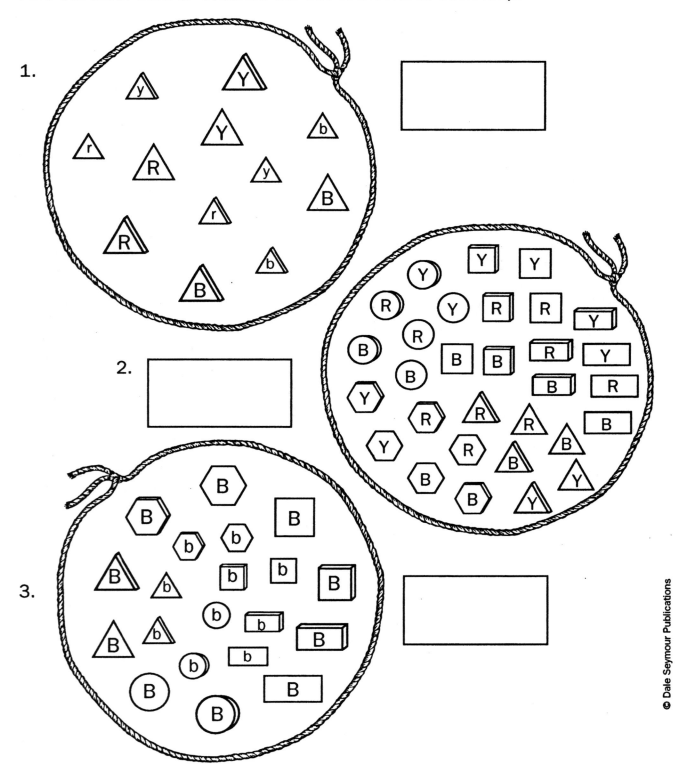

1.

2.

3.

(60-block set)

Name the Set

Activity G

Find the label card to describe the set of blocks in each loop.

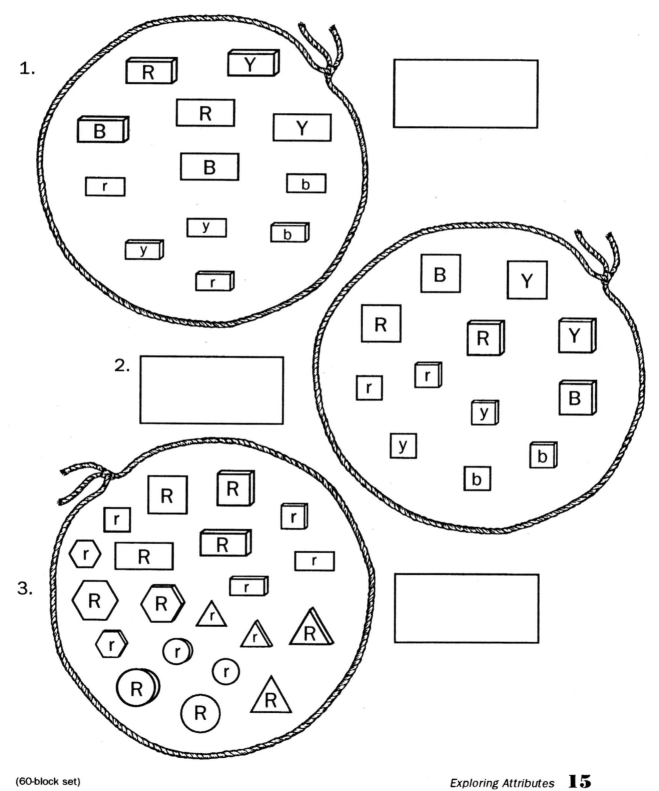

1.

2.

3.

Name the Set

Find the label card to describe the set of blocks in each loop.

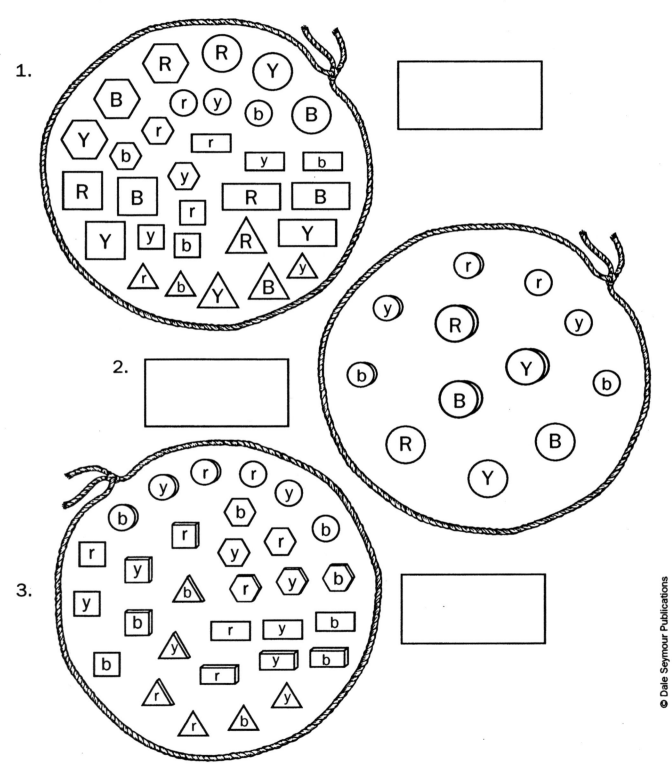

1.

2.

3.

(60-block set)

Name the Set

Activity I

Find a *not* label card to describe the set of blocks in each loop.

1.

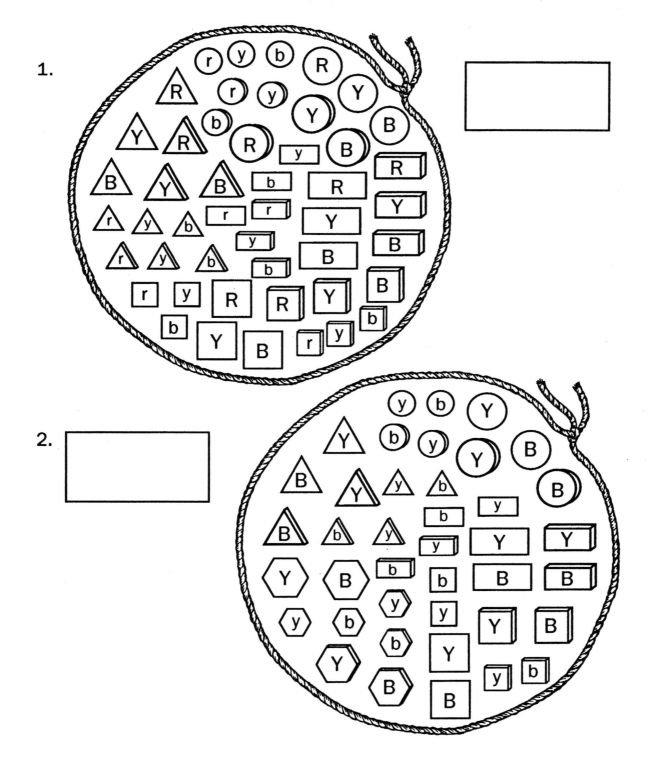

2.

One-Loop Puzzles

Purpose

- To examine the given elements of a pictured set in order to correctly label the set and to determine, through logical thinking, which elements are missing from it.

Materials

- ✔ **One-Loop Puzzles Activity A, B** (pages 19–20), used with 32-block sets and label cards
- ✔ **One-Loop Puzzles Activity C** (page 21), used with 60-block sets and label cards
- ✔ Yarn loop (optional)

Teaching Notes

One-Loop Puzzles, pages 19 to 21, picture only partially filled loops with question marks to indicate that some blocks are missing. Students must determine the missing blocks and the name of the set by looking at the blocks pictured. The number of question marks indicates the number of missing blocks. Students may want to recreate the puzzles pictured on the activity sheets, using a yarn loop and attribute blocks.

Extensions

Using loops of yarn or plain paper on which they draw loops, students can create their own puzzles to challenge their classmates. This is an excellent activity for work in pairs, each student creating a puzzle for the partner to solve. They might use a marker or piece of paper with a "?" on it to represent missing blocks.

The concept of a *subset* of a given set can be discussed. For example, large yellow shapes constitute a subset of the set of yellow shapes. Concretely, we can define a subset by placing a loop containing the large yellow shapes entirely within the loop representing all the yellow shapes. A set is considered a subset of another if all the members of the first set are also in the second set. A subset can have some of the members or all the members of the original set. The set that has no elements (the empty set) is also a subset of every set, since every element in this empty set is also in the original set.

Older students or gifted students can explore some interesting relationships between the number of elements in a set and the number of subsets that set has. This pattern is explained in *Patterns in Pascal's Triangle* by Dale Seymour (Palo Alto, CA: Dale Seymour Publications, 1986).

One-Loop Puzzles

Find the missing blocks and the label cards that describe the sets.

1.

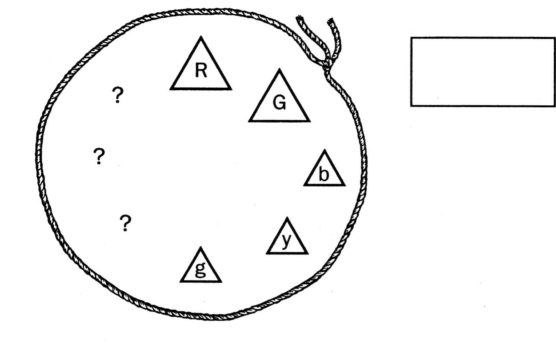

2.

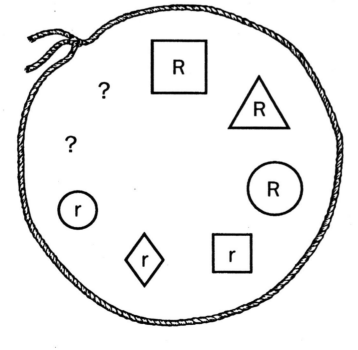

One-Loop Puzzles

Activity B

Find the missing blocks and the label cards that describe the sets.

1.

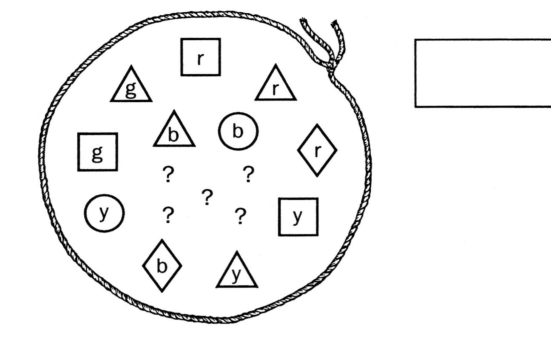

2.

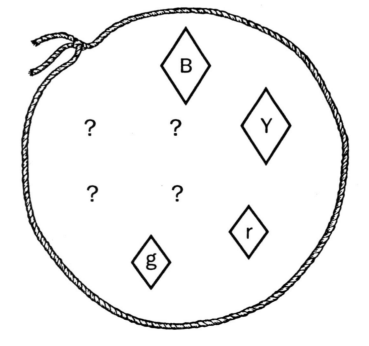

One-Loop Puzzles

Activity C

Find the missing blocks and the label cards that describe the sets.

1.

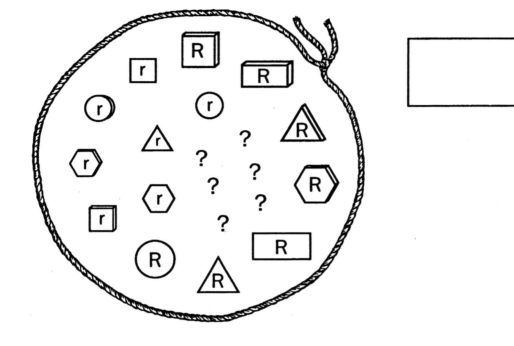

2.

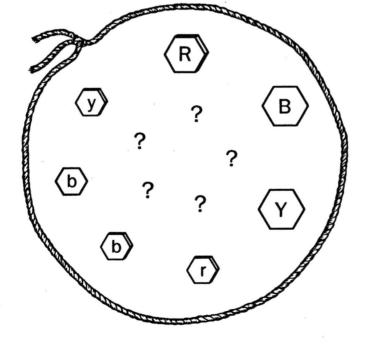

Know Your Blocks

Purpose

- To discover patterns among the number of elements in the various subsets of attribute blocks.

Materials

✔ **Know Your Blocks Activity A, B** (pages 23–24), used with 32-block set

✔ **Know Your Blocks Activity A, C** (pages 23, 25), used with 60-block set

Teaching Notes

On **Know Your Blocks A, B,** and **C,** focus on how many elements are in a set, rather than on which blocks are in the set. These activities will help students when they do the problem-solving applications using Venn diagrams in Section 5.

Encourage younger students to use the actual blocks to verify their answers.

Extensions

You can extend what students have been learning about attributes into a discussion of a *set* as *any group of elements*. The sets that students have been exploring in the attribute blocks each have an obvious, common attribute. However, a group need not have a common attribute in order to be called a set. Any group of elements can be a set. For example, the set of elements "tree, pine cone, sidewalk, grass" might be a set whose common attribute is "in the park." The elements "motherhood, apple pie, and America" also constitute a set.

Ask students to name the elements of sets with a common attribute; for example, "dog, cat, hamster" are in the set "household pets." Then ask them to describe sets in which there is no obvious common attribute.

Ten Questions—a game for two players (or two teams).
This game is played like Twenty Questions, but only ten questions are allowed.

One player secretly selects a mystery block and writes the description of that block on a piece of paper. The challenge is for the other student (or team) to identify the block by asking 10 or fewer yes-no questions.

As the questions are answered, the second player may use the blocks for reference, removing the incorrect blocks from the set until only one block remains.

You may need to encourage younger students to ask more general questions at first rather than questions about a specific block; for example, "Is it blue?" or "Does it have four sides?" rather than "Is it the small green circle?"

Know Your Blocks

Activity A

Sort the blocks by color.

1. How many different sets are there that are named a color?_____

2. If you chose a label card for a color, how many blocks would be in each color set?_____

Sort the blocks by shape.

3. How many different sets are there that are named a shape?_____

4. If you choose the label card for a shape, how many blocks would be in each shape set?_____

Sort the blocks by size.

5. How many different sets are there that are named a size?_____

6. If you choose the label card for a size, how many blocks would be in each size set?_____

7. How many blocks are there in all? _____

8. How many blocks are in the not-square set? _____

9. How many blocks are in the set of large yellow blocks?_____

10. How many blocks are in the set of triangles that are not blue?_____

11. How many blocks are in the set of large circles?_____

12. How many blocks are neither small nor circles?_____

Know Your Blocks

1. How many blocks are in the set of diamonds? _____

2. How many blocks are not-red? _____

3. Name a set of blocks with 16 members. _____

4. Name another set of blocks with 16 members. _____

5. Name two different sets of blocks with 8 members each.

   _____   _____

6. Name two sets of blocks with 4 members each.

   _____

   _____

7. Name two different sets of blocks with 24 members each.

   _____

   _____

8. Name a set of blocks with 12 members.

   _____

9. Name a set of blocks with 1 member.

   _____

(32-block set)

Know Your Blocks

Activity C

1. How many blocks are in the set of triangles? _____

2. How many blocks are in the set of not-red blocks?_____

3. Name a set of blocks with 30 members. _____

4. Name another set of blocks with 30 members._____

5. Name two different sets of blocks with 40 members each.

   _____   _____

6. Name a set of blocks with 5 members.

   _____

7. Name a set of blocks with 1 member.

   _____

8. Name a set of blocks with 48 members.

   _____

9. Name two different sets of blocks with 24 members each.

   _____

   _____

10. Name a set of blocks with 15 members.

   _____

Who Am I?

Purpose

- To develop logical thinking by identifying mystery blocks.

Materials

✔ **Who Am I? Activity A** (page 27), used with 32-block set

✔ **Who Am I? Activity B** (page 28), used with 60-block set

Teaching Notes

The students may need to manipulate the attribute blocks to help them think through the clues. With each new clue, they can remove the inappropriate blocks from consideration. For younger students, plan to read aloud the clues, or ask a capable reader to do so.

Discuss with students which clues were the most helpful in finding the mystery piece? To save copying, laminate and reuse copies of these and other activities in this book. Students can record their answers in a math notebook.

Students can make up their own problems and challenge fellow students to discover the mystery block.

Extensions

Name the Block—a card game for three or four players.

Use index cards or the blackline masters for the label cards (page x or xii) to create a deck of playing cards. With the 32-block set, you will need a deck of 40 cards; with the 60-block set, 48 cards. Each deck should contain four cards each of the following labels:

For the 32-block set: blue, red, yellow, green, □, ○, △, ◇, large, small

For the 60-block set: blue, red, yellow, □, ▭, ○, △, ◯, large, small, thick, thin.

- To begin, the dealer chooses one block and places it in the center of the table, then shuffles the cards and deals four cards face down to each player. One card is placed face up, starting a discard pile. The remaining deck forms a draw pile.

- The player to the left of the dealer draws first. A turn consists of selecting one card from either the draw or discard pile and then discarding one card. Play moves clockwise.

- The winner of the hand is the first player to display the three or four cards that completely describe the block.

Who Am I?

1. I am not large nor am I yellow.
   I have more than three sides.
   I am not blue or green.
   I am not a diamond.

   Who am I? _____

2. I am not large.
   I am green or red.
   Like a doughnut, I have no corners.
   I am not red.

   Who am I? _____

3. I am small.
   I have corners, but fewer than four.
   I am not red, or yellow, or green.

   Who am I? _____

4. I am quite large.
   I am not green.
   The number of my sides rhymes with score.
   I am neither red nor blue.
   I am not a square.

   Who am I? _____

5. I am neither yellow nor blue.
   I have corners but not as many as a square.
   I am not small nor am I green.

   Who am I? _____

6. On separate paper create your own **Who Am I?** puzzle.

Who Am I?

1. I am small, but not thin.
   I have more than three sides, but fewer than six.
   I am yellow.
   I am not a square.

   Who am I? _____

2. I have more than three sides, all the same length.
   I am the color of a stop sign.
   I am large, but not thick.
   I am not a square.

   Who am I? _____

3. I have no corners.
   I am not thick.
   I am neither red nor yellow
   I am small.

   Who am I? _____

4. I am thick and large.
   Each of my sides is the same length.
   I am blue.
   I have four sides.

   Who am I? _____

5. I have more than four corners.
   I am not yellow.
   I am large and thick.
   I am not blue.

   Who am I? _____

6. On separate paper create your own **Who Am I?** puzzle.

SECTION

2

Making Patterns

What Comes Next?

Purpose

- To recognize and extend patterns governing sequences made with the attribute blocks.

Materials

✔ **What Comes Next? Activity A, B, C** (pages 31–33), used with 32-block set

✔ **What Comes Next? Activity C, D, E** (pages 33–35), used with 60-block set

Teaching Notes

Introduce this activity by building a sequence with attribute blocks. Demonstrate to the students how blocks are placed one by one in a special pattern. For example starting with red shapes alternate large then small of different shapes in order, then begin on a new color and follow the same pattern of shapes.

Ask students to continue the pattern and then describe in words a rule that governs the sequence pictured. They can express the rule orally or write the rule for each pattern in their notebook.

Encourage students to place the actual blocks on top of the activity sheets as they work to discover the pattern.

In some patterns, such as **What Comes Next? Activity A**, pattern 1, there is only one choice for the next block. Once that block is placed, however, there are several choices for the next block. It can be the large red block of a different shape, or the large green square block. In other patterns, such as **What Comes Next? Activity B**, pattern 1, there is only one choice for each subsequent block. Enough of the pattern is shown to determine the pattern for the colors (red, green, yellow, blue), the pattern for the shapes (triangle, square, circle), and the pattern for the size (large, small).

Encourage students to talk and write about patterns that can be completed in just one way and those that can be completed in more than one way.

Extensions

Ask students to generate their own patterns with rules and then challenge their classmates to complete the pattern and state the rule. For some students it is easier to verbally describe the pattern than to put the blocks into a pattern.

What Comes Next?

Activity A

1.

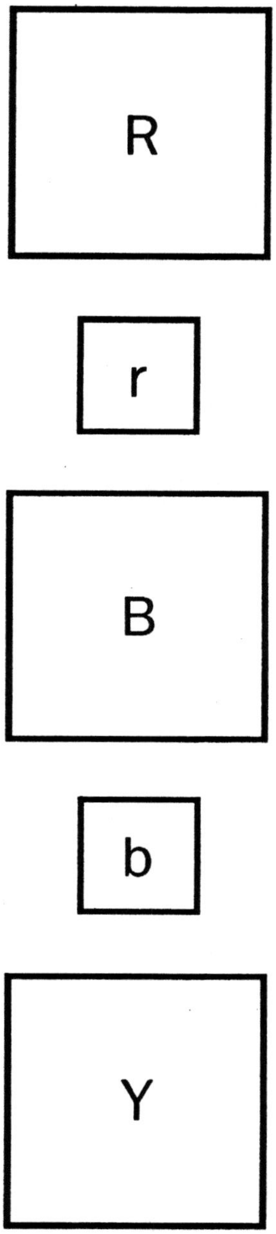

R

r

B

b

Y

2.

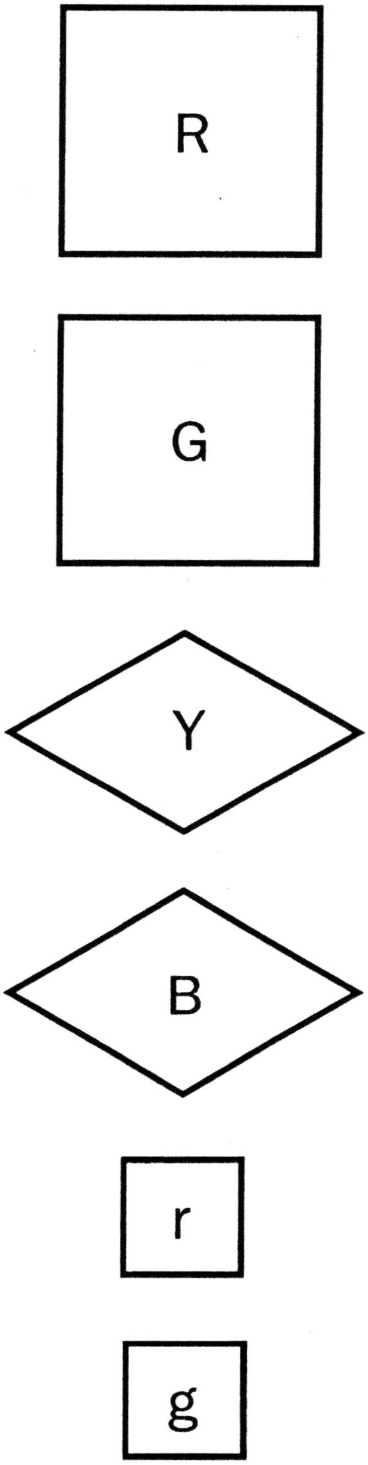

R

G

Y

B

r

g

What Comes Next?

Activity B

1.

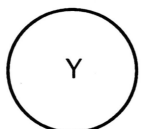

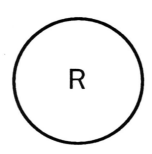

2.

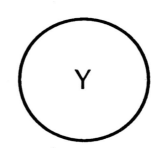

(32- or 60-block set)

What Comes Next?

Activity C

1.

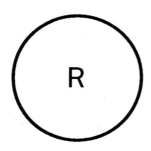

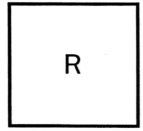

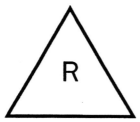

2.

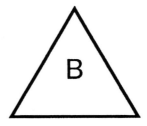

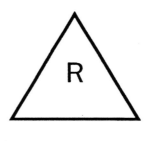

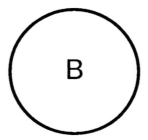

What Comes Next?

Activity D

1.

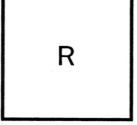

R

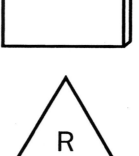

R

R

R

R

2.

R

B

Y

R

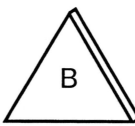

B

(60-block set)

What Comes Next?

Activity E

1.

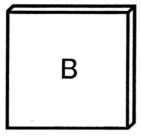

r

R

b

2.

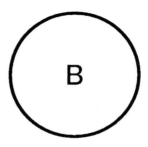

y

R

y

B

y

Complete the Arrangement

Purpose

- To recognize and extend patterns governing arrays of attribute blocks.

Materials

- ✔ **Complete the Arrangement Activity A, B, C** (pages 37–39), used with 32-block set
- ✔ **Complete the Arrangement Activity D, E, F** (pages 40–42), used with 60-block set

Teaching Notes

Before introducing the activity sheets, begin with a small-group activity. Give each student a set of attribute blocks. Ask the students to arrange some of their blocks. Then direct all the students to close their eyes while you remove one block from one of the arrangements. When you give the signal, the students open their eyes and try to determine which block is missing.

As this challenge moves from one student's arrangement to another, the group should recognize that patterns make it easier to determine the missing block.

Now direct the students to arrange some of their blocks in an array of rows and columns. Again have them identify the block you removed from the array while their eyes were closed. Students who use patterns in both the rows and the columns will find it easy to determine the missing block.

On **Complete the Arrangement Activity A** through **Activity F**, the students must identify several missing blocks in an array of rows and columns. To determine which blocks are missing, the students must look for patterns in both the horizontal and vertical directions. Sometimes more than one attribute is changing across a row or down a column. Students may recreate the array with attribute blocks and then complete the pattern.

Extensions

Using the attribute blocks, students create their own **Complete the Arrangement** puzzles. A 4-by-4 or 2-by-4 grid can be used for the 32-block set. For the 60-block set, many grids can be used, including 5 by 3, 5 by 4, 5 by 6, 4 by 4, or 3 by 4, depending on which attributes are involved in each pattern. Make blank grids on large paper so that the actual attribute blocks will fit in the cells.

Students might work in small groups, with one student first secretly generating a pattern and then removing some of the blocks. The other students in the group are then challenged to discover the missing blocks and to describe the rules that govern the arrangement.

Complete the Arrangement

Activity A

Y (square)			Y (diamond)
		B (circle)	
	R (triangle)		
	G (triangle)		

Complete the Arrangement

Activity B

(R)			(G)
	(b)	(y)	
△R			
			△g

(32-block set)

Complete the Arrangement

Activity C

b		g	
	B		G
		g	
			G

Complete the Arrangement

Activity D

(60-block set)

Complete the Arrangement

Activity E

r			R
	R		
		r	
r			
			R

(60-block set)

Complete the Arrangement

Activity F

		y	y
△ r			
	⬡ r		
	◯ r	◯ y	
▢ r			y

(60-block set)

SECTION 3

Difference Activities

How Am I Different?

Purpose

- To develop logical thinking by comparing blocks according to likenesses and differences.

Materials

✔ **How Am I Different? Activity A, C** (pages 45, 47), used with 32-block set and difference cards

✔ **How Am I Different? Activity B, C** (pages 46–47), used with 60-block set and difference cards

Teaching Notes

Use the first example on **How Am I Different? Activity A** (for the 32-block set) and **Activity B** (for the 60-block set) to introduce the idea that we can compare blocks by looking at ways in which blocks are alike and different. After discussing the example, direct students to find blocks that differ from given blocks in a specified number of ways, and to indicate how each pair of blocks is different and how it is alike. Students should recognize that the blocks may differ in one, two, or three ways in the 32-block set, and may differ in one, two, three, or four ways in the 60-block set.

On **How Am I Different? Activity C**, students are asked to find all of the blocks that are different in one (two, or more) way(s) from a given block.

Start with blocks that are different in one way from the small (thin) blue circle. Students may take different approaches to this problem. Some may select one block at a time, compare it to the small (thin) blue circle, and decide if their selected block is different from the original block in exactly one way. Other students may focus on a single attribute at a time, thinking, for example: "We can change the color, but keep the same size and shape (and thickness); then we can change the size, but keep the other attributes the same."

Using different combinations of the reproducible attribute cards and difference cards (pages xi–xiv) on **How Am I Different? Activity C**, you can reproduce this mat to make many different reusable activity sheets.

Questions for discussion. If two blocks are different in two ways, in how many ways are they alike? How would you describe the blocks not selected?

Extensions

Students can work in pairs, with one student choosing a block and the other choosing a difference card. Then they can take turns choosing blocks that fit the description, verbalizing the ways each block is the same as the given block and the ways it is different, and checking each other as they work.

How Am I Different?

These blocks are different in one way—size.
They are alike in two ways—color and shape.

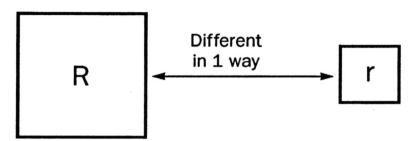

Different
in 1 way

Find a block to compare to each block below and complete the
sentences to describe the comparison.

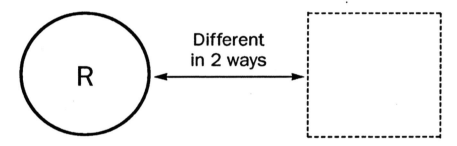

Different
in 2 ways

These blocks are different in two ways— _____ and _____.

They are alike in one way— _____.

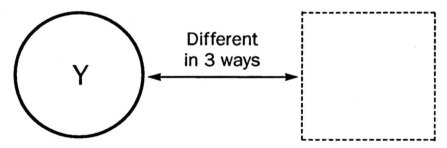

Different
in 3 ways

These blocks are different in three ways—_____,

_____, and _____.

They are not alike in any way.

How Am I Different?

Activity B

These blocks are different in one way—size.
They are alike in three ways—color, thickness, and shape.

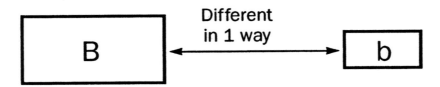

Find a block to compare to each block below and complete the sentences to describe the comparison.

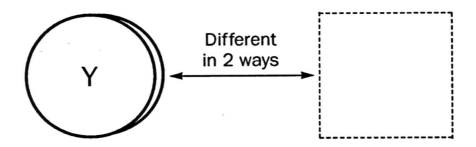

These blocks are different in two ways— _____ and _____.

They are alike in two ways _____ and _____.

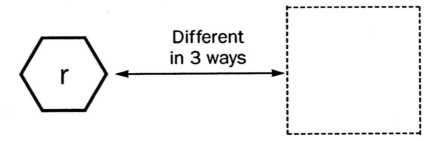

These blocks are different in three ways—_____ , _____ ,

and _____.

They are alike in one way—_____.

(60-block set)

How Am I Different?

Activity C

Place one block here.

Place a difference card here.

Place the blocks here that differ from the one above in the number of ways indicated on the difference card.

Difference Trains

Purpose

- To develop logical thinking by comparing blocks according to likenesses and differences.

Materials

✔ **Difference Trains Activity A, B, C** (pages 49–51), used with 32-block set and difference cards

✔ **Difference Trains Activity A, D, E** (pages 49, 52–53), used with 60-block set and difference cards

Teaching Notes

Introduce this activity at the concrete level. Ask a student to choose any block; explain that this is the engine of a train. Ask another student to continue the train by choosing a second block that differs from the first block in exactly one way. Place the second block next to the first block as the first car. Ask another student to place a third car on the train, choosing a block that differs from the second block in exactly one way. Continue the train in this manner. As each block is chosen, ask the students to describe the way each pair of adjoining blocks is different, and the ways they are the same.

Questions for Discussion. Could we bring the beginning and end of the train together to form a circle? If we do this, is the one-difference rule between blocks maintained? Could we exchange specific blocks in the train and still maintain the one-difference rule? Can you break the train into two segments and arrange it in an X, with one block as the pivot point? Is the one-difference rule between the blocks maintained?

Once the students understand the concept of making a train, use **Difference Trains Activity A** to introduce the activity sheet format. Use the difference cards to indicate the number of differences there should be between adjacent blocks. This sheet can be reproduced with each of the difference cards to make a variety of reusable difference train activities. Subsequent activity sheets challenge students to complete trains already started. The students can record their solutions either by placing the actual blocks on the train or by drawing in coded or colored pictures.

Extensions

Encourage individual students to use the blocks to make one-, two-, or three-difference trains, then challenge fellow students to identify which type of train has been made.

Difference Trains

Activity A

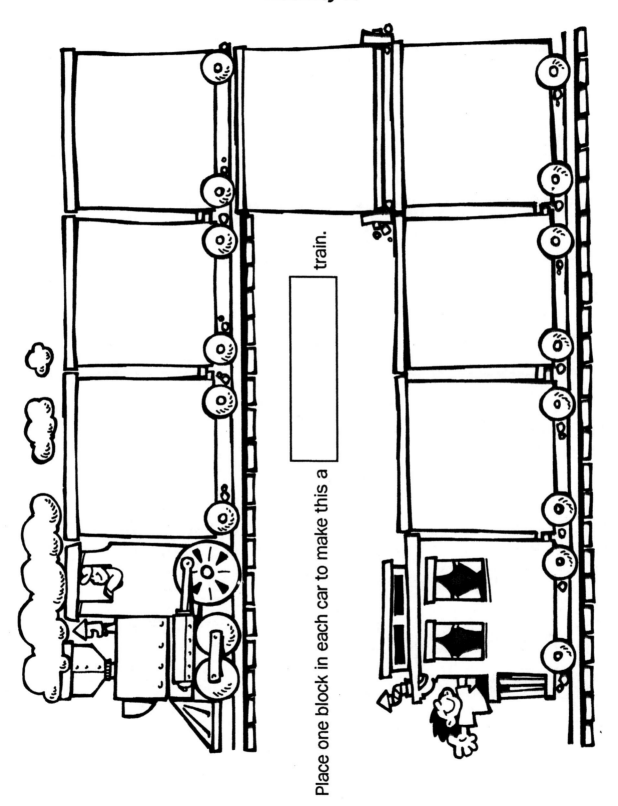

Place one block in each car to make this a _____ train.

(32- or 60-block set)

Difference Trains

Activity B

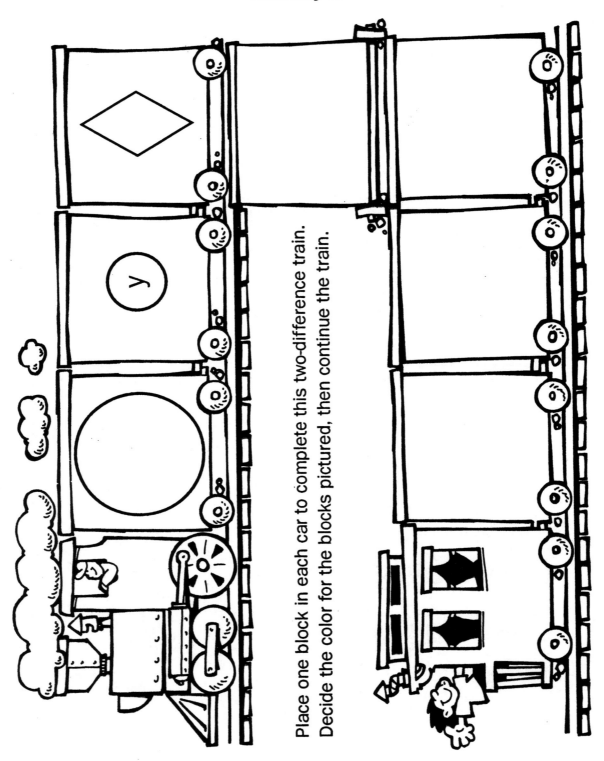

Place one block in each car to complete this two-difference train.
Decide the color for the blocks pictured, then continue the train.

© Dale Seymour Publications

(32-block set)

Difference Trains

Activity C

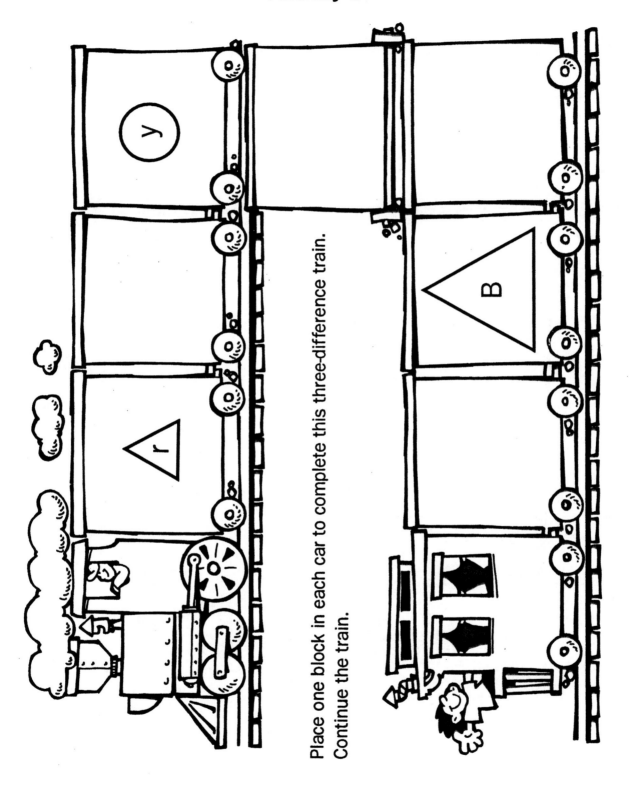

Place one block in each car to complete this three-difference train. Continue the train.

Difference Trains

Activity D

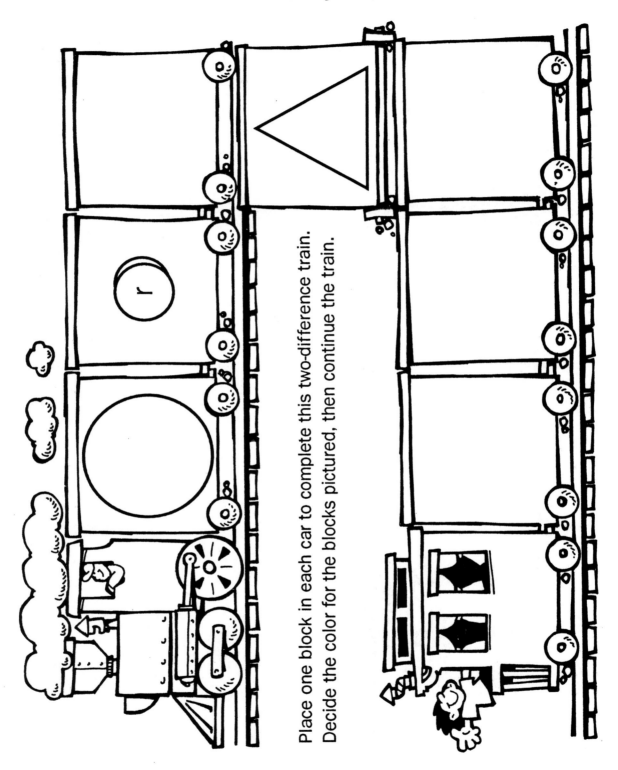

Place one block in each car to complete this two-difference train. Decide the color for the blocks pictured, then continue the train.

Difference Trains

Activity E

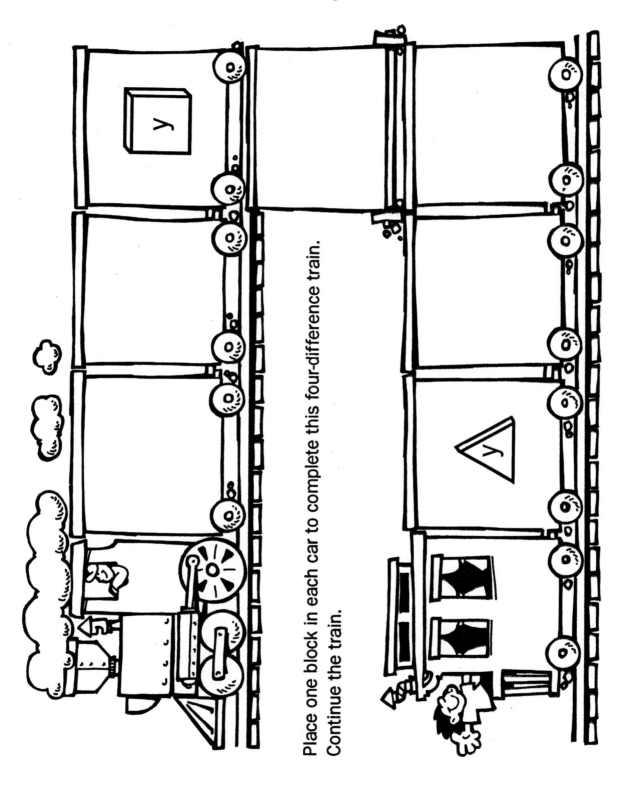

Place one block in each car to complete this four-difference train. Continue the train.

Follow the Arrows

Purpose

- To extend logical thinking by arranging blocks so that they differ in specified ways from one or more blocks.

Materials

✔ **Follow the Arrows Activity A, B, C** (pages 55–57), used with 32- or 60-block set

Teaching Notes

The **Follow the Arrows** activity sheets deal with specified differences that must be considered simultaneously, sometimes with more than two blocks in mind.

Follow the Arrows Activity A specifies a block in the START position. **Follow the Arrows Activity B** offers a more open format, where the student chooses the block for the initial position. Some students may find it easier not to place the first block in the top START position, but rather to work backwards from the center position.

Follow the Arrows Activity C is more difficult, since the attribute to be changed is unspecified. This activity lets the student choose the starting block and indicates the number or differences (but not what the difference is) between blocks.

Questions for Discussion. When a block is given in the START position, is there only one solution? Which position in each of the diagrams is the most difficult to fill? Why?

Extensions

Ask the students to create their own difference challenges. Before students trade challenges with other students, they must provide solutions to each challenge they create.

Follow the Arrows

Activity A

Start with the small red triangle. Follow an arrow to another position and put another block in the new position. The new block must be different from its neighbor according to the description on the arrow.

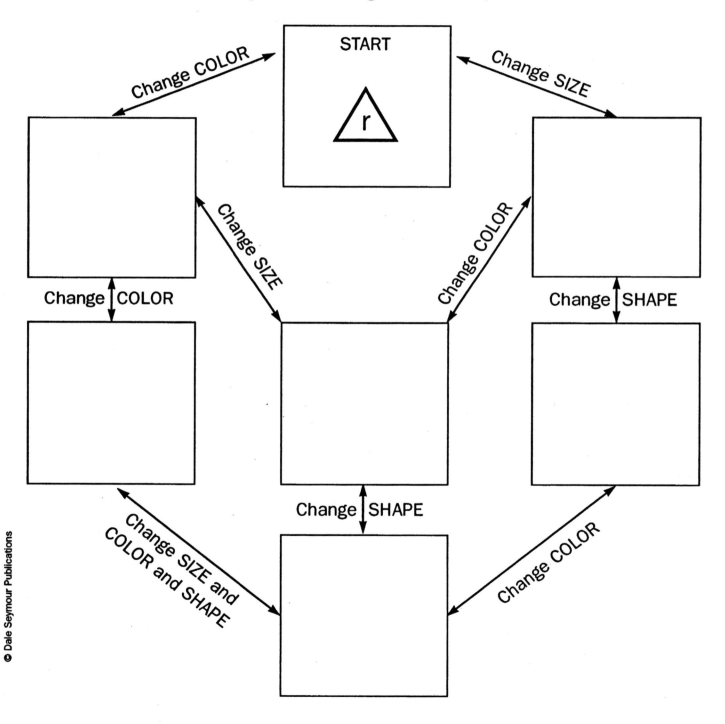

Follow the Arrows

Activity B

Put a block in START. Follow an arrow to another position and put another block in the new position. The new block must be different from its neighbor according to the description on the arrow.

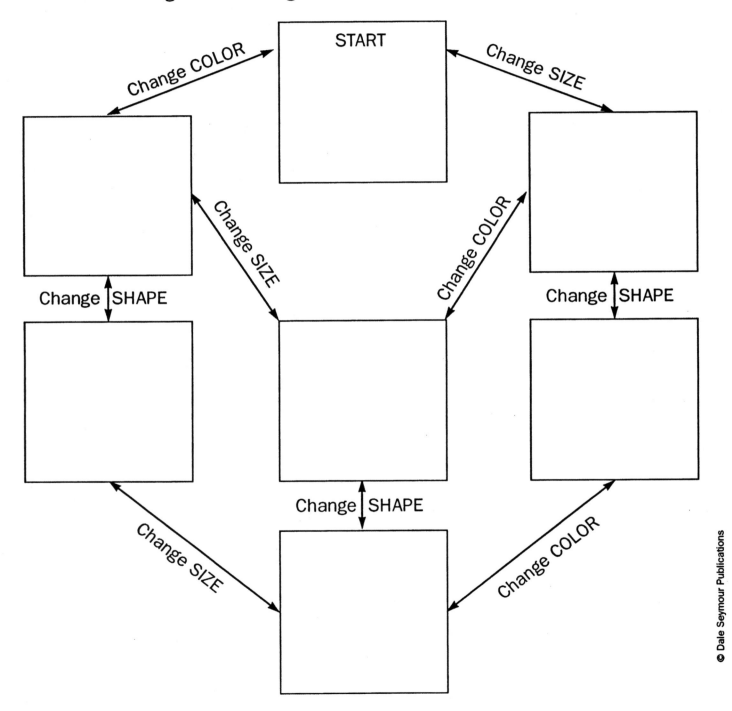

(32- or 60-block set)

Follow the Arrows

Activity C

Put a block on START. Follow an arrow to another position and put another block in the new position. The new block must be different from its neighbor in the number of ways indicated on the arrow.

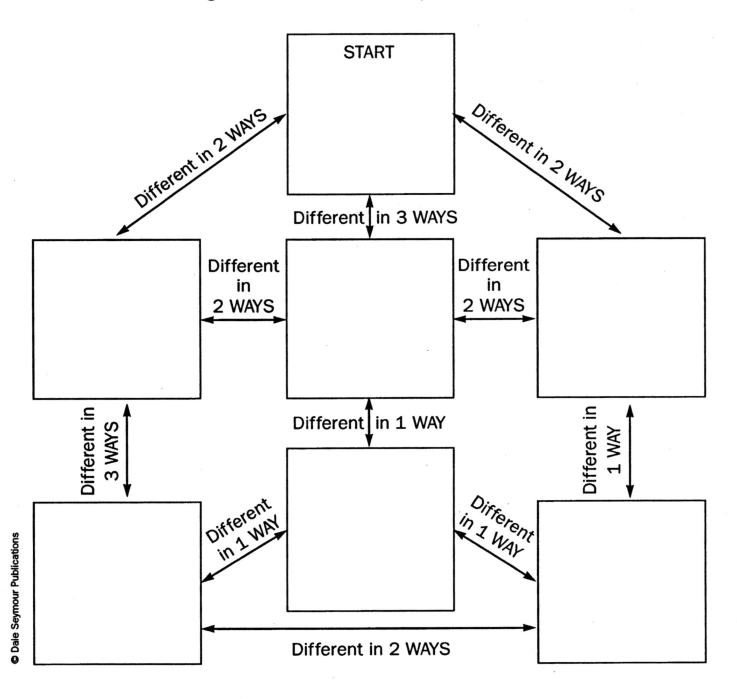

START

Different in 2 WAYS

Different in 2 WAYS

Different in 3 WAYS

Different in 2 WAYS

Different in 2 WAYS

Different in 3 WAYS

Different in 1 WAY

Different in 1 WAY

Different in 1 WAY

Different in 1 WAY

Different in 2 WAYS

Different in Both Directions

Purpose

- To use logical thinking and problem-solving strategies to solve two-dimensional puzzles involving one-, two-, and three-attribute differences.

Materials

✔ **Different in Both Directions Activity A, B, C, D, E, F** (pages 59–64), used with 32- or 60-block set

Teaching Notes

These activities offer a variety of two-dimensional formats—2-by-2 and 3-by-3 difference arrays, as well as an "I" shape.

On **Different in Both Directions Activity A** through **E**, specific blocks have already been placed, and students are challenged to fill in the rest according to the number of differences specified. Students may color in the pictured shapes or cover them with the corresponding blocks to make the activity more concrete.

Different in Both Directions Activity F can be used with various difference cards to create additional puzzles (either teacher- or student-made).

Be sure the students understand that specified differences must be considered for adjoining blocks both horizontally and vertically. However, the blocks need not follow the difference rule in the diagonal direction.

Questions for Discussion. Does it matter where you start? Once you have a complete array, can you replace a single block somewhere and maintain the differences specified?

Extensions

Students can create their own difference arrays that use square or rectangular grids of varying dimensions. Ask them to create a difference array and then remove some of the blocks. Ask another student to complete it again. Were the same blocks used as were used in the original difference array?

Ask the students to complete any of the activity sheets using *only* the large or *only* the small blocks.

Different in Both Directions

This is a one-difference array. Place the blocks on the difference array so that each block is different from its horizontal and vertical neighbor in exactly one way.

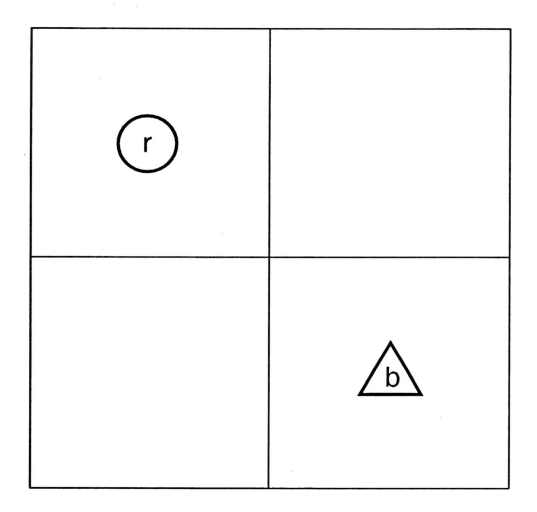

Make this a two-difference array so that each block is different from its neighbors in two ways.

Different in Both Directions

Activity B

This is a two-difference I. Place the blocks on the difference I so that each block is different from its horizontal and vertical neighbor in exactly two ways.

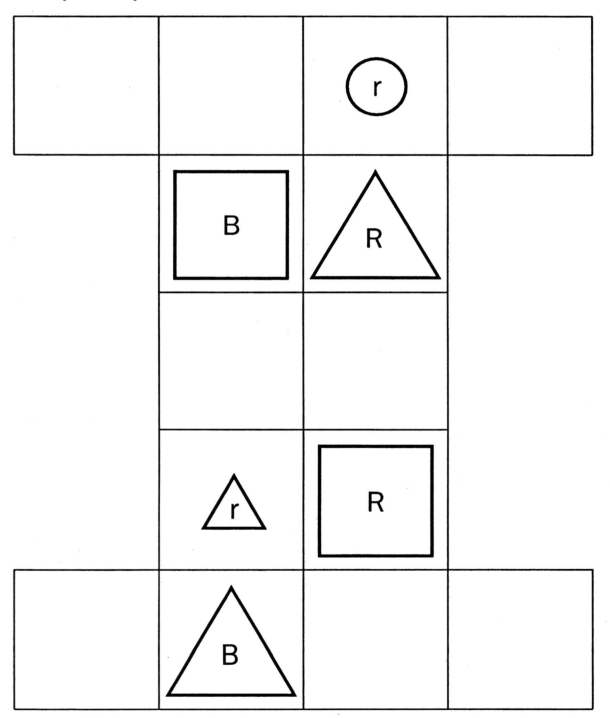

© Dale Seymour Publications

Different in Both Directions

This is a three-difference array. Place the blocks on the difference array so that each block is different from its horizontal and vertical neighbor in exactly three ways.

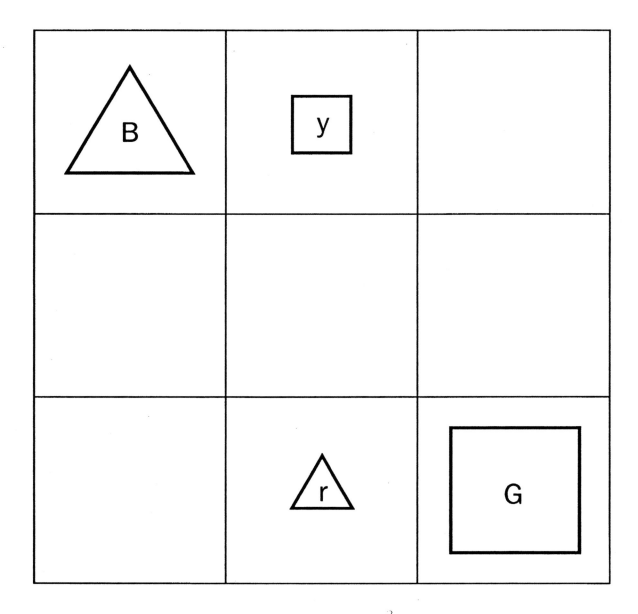

Different in Both Directions

This is a two-difference array. Place the blocks on the difference array so that each block is different from its horizontal and vertical neighbor in exactly two ways.

	(r)	[y]
[Y]	△y	(Y)
(y)		

Different in Both Directions

Activity E

This is a three-difference array. Place the blocks on the difference array so that each block is different from its horizontal and vertical neighbor in exactly three ways.

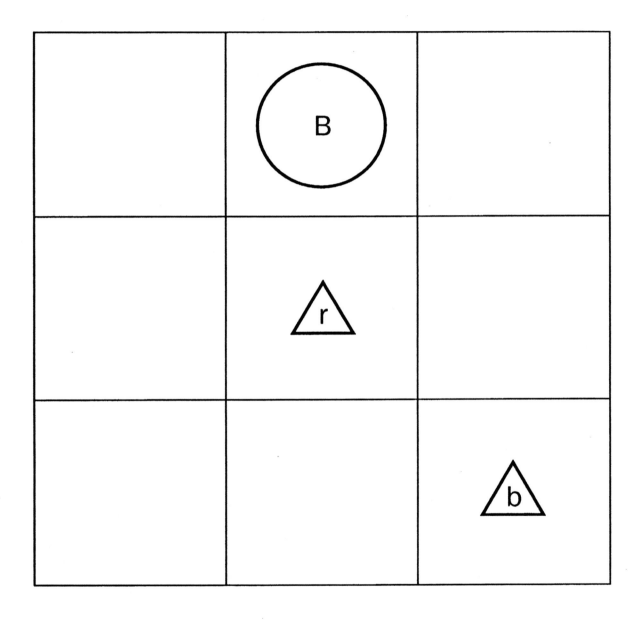

Different in Both Directions

Activity F

This is a [_____] array. Fill in the missing blocks.

SECTION

4

Loop Activities

Two-Loop Sorting

Purpose

- To introduce the concepts of union and intersections of sets using Venn diagrams

Materials

✔ **Two-Loop Sorting** (page 67), or yarn loops, used with 32- or 60-block set and label cards

Teaching Notes

Introduce **Two-Loop Sorting** in a small group using blocks. Place two yarn loops beside each other on the table, but not overlapping. Select two label cards that describe sets with no common blocks, for example, blue and red.

Ask the students to place the attribute blocks where they belong: either inside one of the loops, or outside the loops on the table. Check to see that all blocks are properly placed.

Next, select a pair of label cards that describe sets that share some elements, such as blue and triangle. Place the label cards on the two separate loops, and ask the students to place the blocks in the correct loop.

Let the students discover the concept of intersection by leading a discussion along these lines:

Teacher: Do you have all the blue pieces inside the loop labeled blue?
Student: Yes.
Teacher: Good. Let's look at the other loop. Are all the triangles in it?
Student: No.
Teacher: Which ones are missing?
Student: The blue ones.

Ask one of the students to move the blue triangles to the triangle loop.

Teacher: The triangle loop is now complete. Let's check the other loop again.

Encourage the students to conclude that, to deal with two sets simultaneously, the best arrangement is overlapping circles with a region that represents the intersection of the two sets.

Extensions

- Use label cards for sets that don't overlap and discuss the result.
- Use the not label cards.

Two-Loop Sorting

Activity A

Sort the blocks according to the labels.

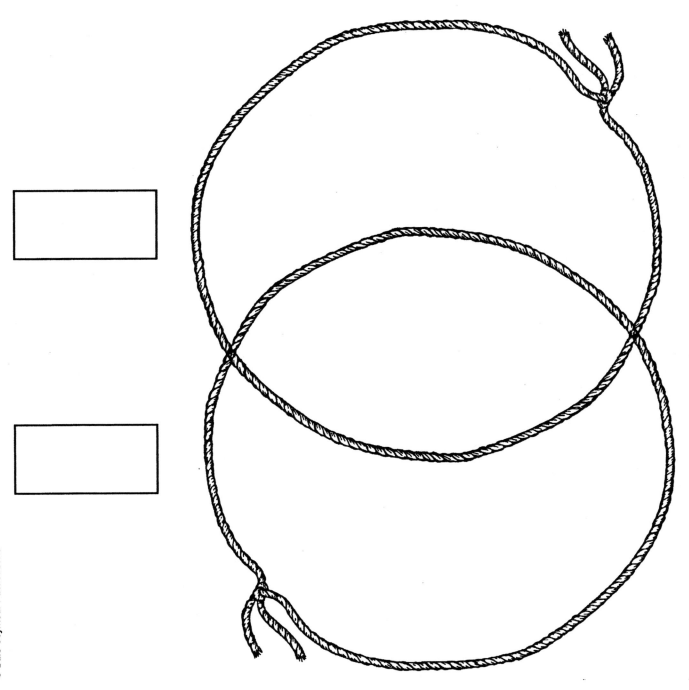

Two-Loop Puzzles

Purpose

- To name sets by examining their union and intersection represented in Venn diagrams.

Materials

✔ **Two-Loop Puzzles Activity A, B, C** (pages 69–71), used with 32-block set and label cards

✔ **Two-Loop Puzzles Activity D, E,** (pages 72–73), used with 60-block set and label cards

✔ Yarn loops (optional)

Teaching Notes

Two-Loop Puzzles give students further practice in reverse processing; that is, given the elements of sets, the students must name the sets. This activity helps students develop problem solving and critical thinking strategies.

Some students may find it helpful to use yarn loops and the actual blocks to recreate the sets pictured on the activity sheets.

Focus students' attention on the two sets with questions such as the following:

Which blocks are in both sets?
Which blocks are in neither set?
Which blocks are only in the set _____?
Which blocks are in either set?

Extensions

In the Loops—a game for two players (or two teams).

Use **Two-Loop Sorting** (page 67) or two overlapping yarn or rigid loops as the playing mat.

- Shuffle the label cards and place them face down in the center of the table.

- The first player selects two label cards, looks at them without showing the other player, and then places them face down, one on each loop.

- The second player chooses a block and tries to locate the region of the loops where it belongs. After several blocks have been placed correctly and there are enough clues, the second player tries to identify the sets named on the label cards.

- Players then reverse roles.

- The goal is to identify the two sets with the fewest number of blocks placed.

Two-Loop Puzzles

Activity A

Find the label cards that describe the sets.

1.

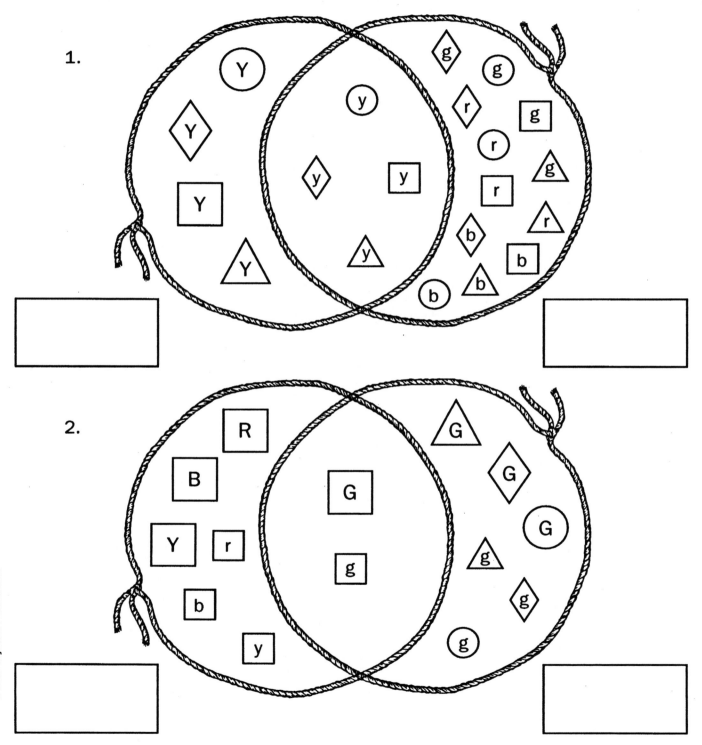

2.

Two-Loop Puzzles

Activity B

Find the label cards that describe the sets.

1.

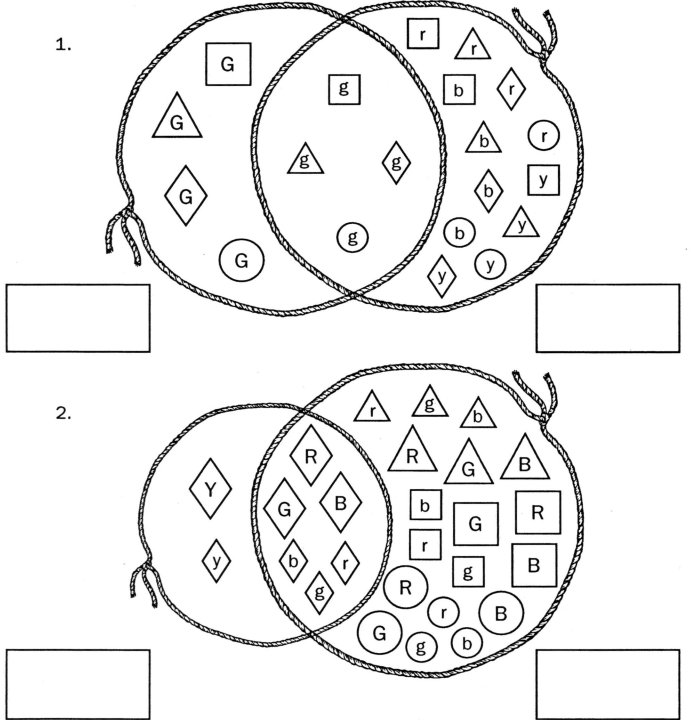

2.

(32-block set)

Two-Loop Puzzles

Activity C

Find the label cards that describe the sets.

1.

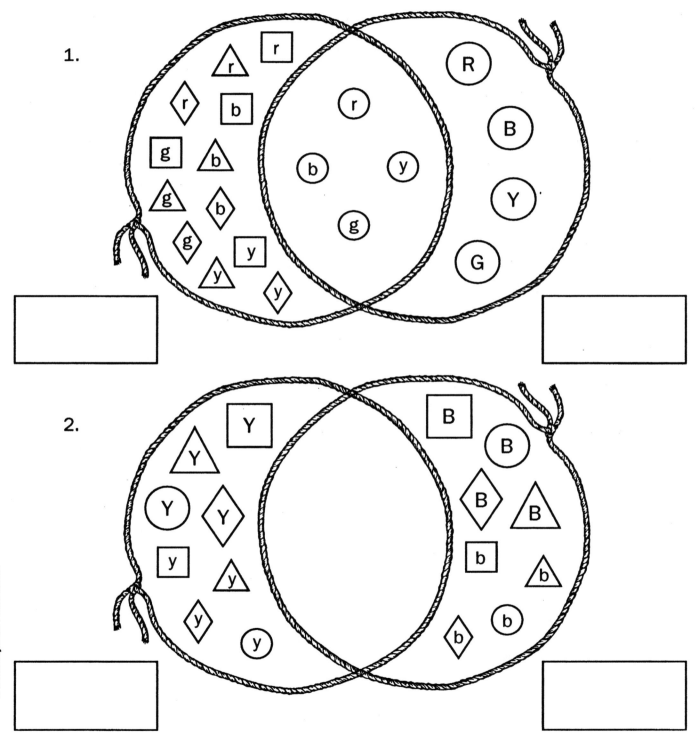

2.

Two-Loop Puzzles

Activity D

Find the label cards that describe the sets.

1.

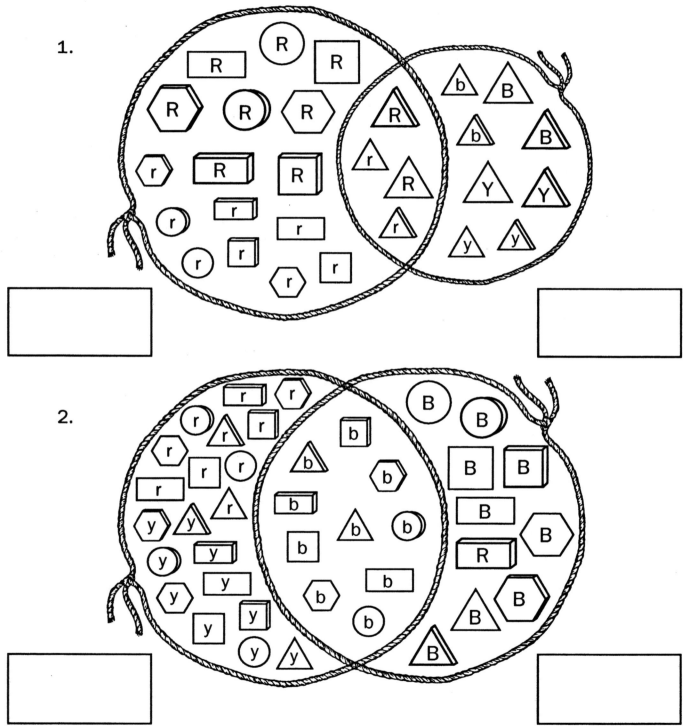

2.

(60-block set)

Two-Loop Puzzles

Activity E

Find the label cards that describe the sets.

1.

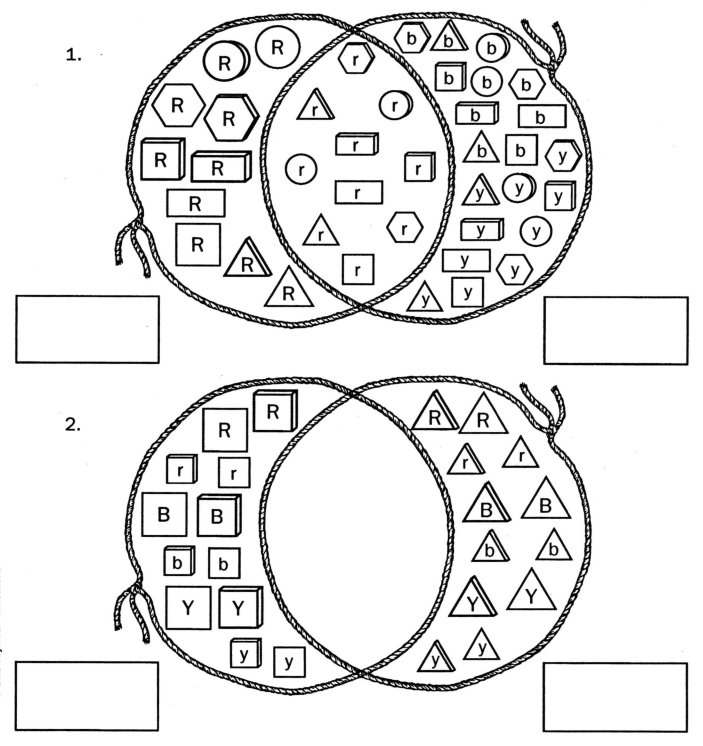

2.

Two-Loop Mysteries

Purpose

- To examine sets represented in Venn diagrams, correctly label them, and determine missing elements using logical thinking.

Materials

✔ **Two-Loop Mysteries Activity A, B** (pages 75–76), used with 32-block set and label cards

✔ **Two-Loop Mysteries Activity C** (page 77), used with 60-block set and label cards

Teaching Notes

Two-Loop Mysteries extend the **Two-Loop Puzzle** activities by presenting intersecting sets without label cards and with certain blocks missing. Students must analyze the blocks pictured and determine what set it is and which blocks are missing. Each question mark stands for a missing block.

As with the **Two-Loop Puzzles**, some students may find the problems easier to solve if they recreate the pictured sets using loops and the attribute blocks.

The solutions to these exercises on page 129 list first the names of the attributes of the two sets and then the blocks that go with the ?'s. The blocks listed before the first semicolon are those that belong in the left-hand region of the diagram; next the ?'s in the intersection are listed; finally those in the region to the far right are listed.

Extensions

Students can create their own puzzles to challenge their classmates using either the **Two-Loop Sorting** sheet (page 67), plain paper on which they construct their own loops, or loops of yarn. This is an excellent activity for work in pairs, with each student creating a puzzle for the other to solve.

Two-Loop Mysteries

Activity A

Find the missing blocks and the label cards that describe the sets.

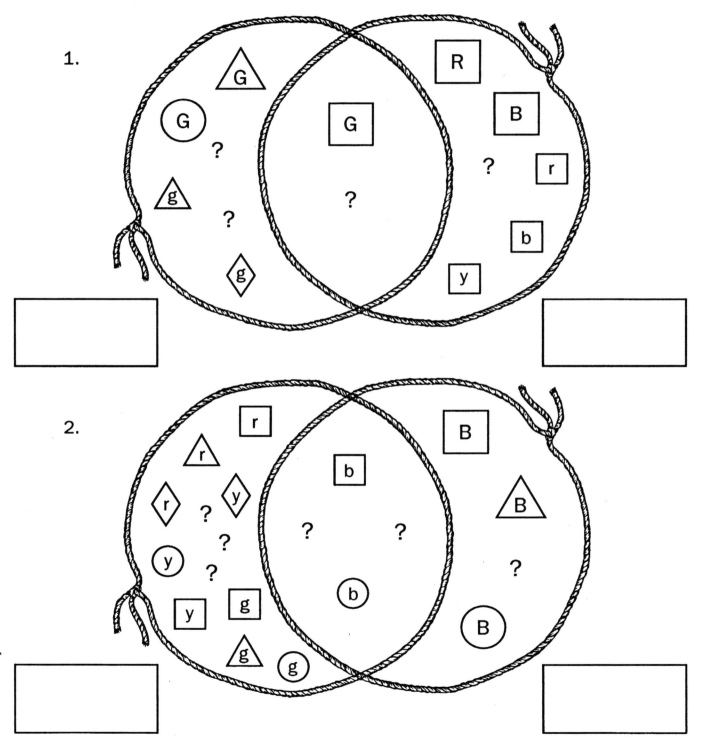

1.

2.

Two-Loop Mysteries

Activity B

Find the missing blocks and the label cards that describe the sets.

1.

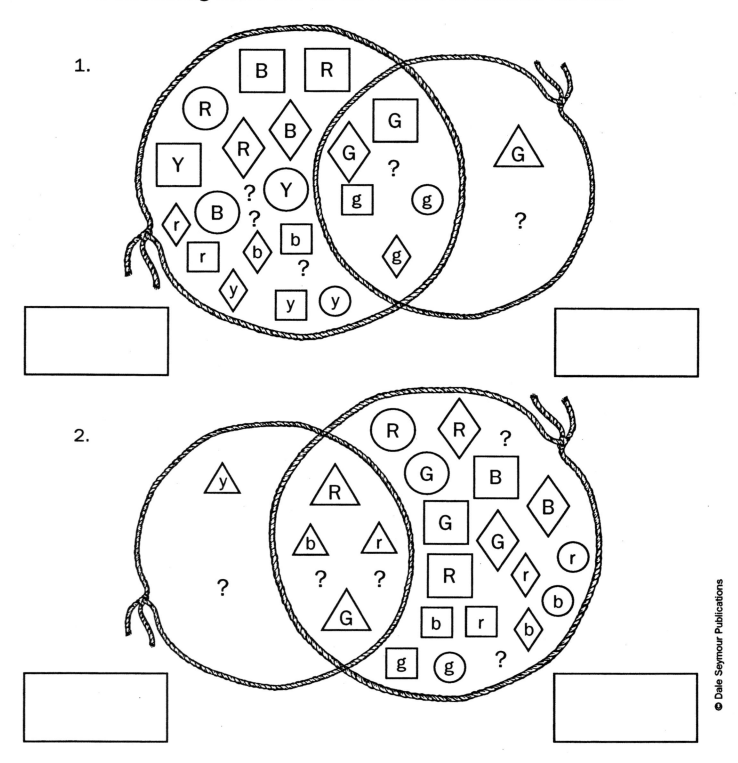

2.

(32-block set)

Two-Loop Mysteries

Activity C

Find the missing blocks and the label cards that describe the sets.

1.

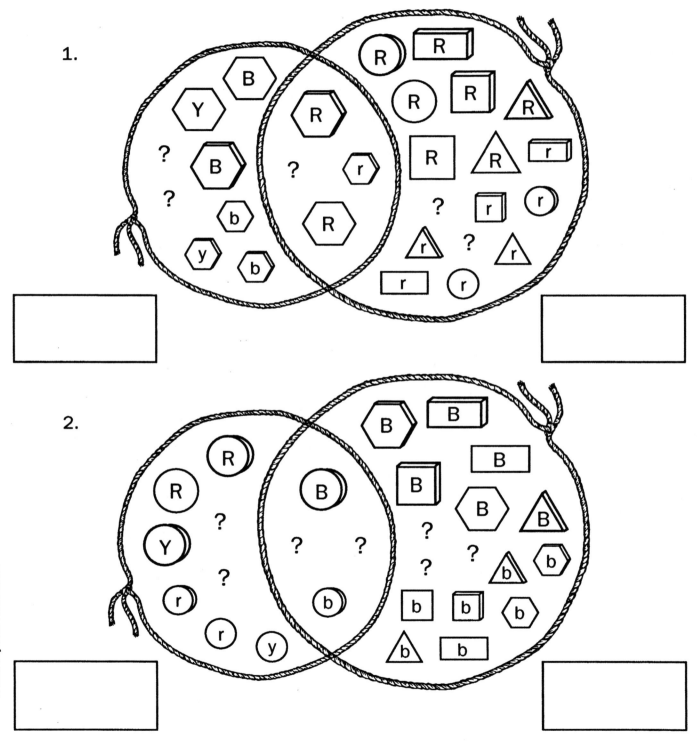

2.

Three-Loop Sorting

Purpose

- To extend the understanding of intersections and unions of sets to three sets represented by Venn diagrams.

Materials

✔ **Three-Loop Sorting** (page 79)

✔ Rigid loops or yarn loops used with 32- or 60-block set and label cards

Teaching Notes

Introduce **Three-Loop Sorting** with a concrete experience, using the rigid (or yarn) loops and the blocks.

Start by posing a basic two-loop problem, such as blue and square. By now, students should have no trouble placing the blocks appropriately.

Next, ask the students to place another loop on this arrangement, label it large, and place all the large blocks in this third loop. Using an inquiry approach similar to that described for **Two-Loop Sorting** (page 66), guide students to discover the three-loop arrangement for this problem.

When the arrangement is complete, help students understand the meaning of the different regions by asking them to describe the blocks in each part of the diagram. Ask questions like the following:

How many blocks are blue and square and large? (32—1 block, 60—2 blocks)

How many blocks are either blue or square or large? (32—the 23 blocks inside any part of the three circles, 60—44 blocks)

How many blocks are blue but not square? (32—6 blocks, 60—16 blocks)

How many blocks are both square and blue? (32—2 blocks, 60—4 blocks)

How many blocks are blue but neither square nor large? (32—3 blocks, 60—8 blocks)

Use large rigid loops, the attribute blocks, and the label cards to create and solve problems. Shuffle the label cards and place one on each loop. For some combinations of label cards, no blocks will be in the intersecting circles.

Three-Loop Sorting presents another three-loop Venn diagram; using the questions as a guide, encourage students to talk about the number of elements in the different regions.

Extensions

Use the not label cards to create more challenging problems.

Ask the students to shuffle the label cards and draw three to create a three-loop problem. Discuss which combinations of cards give empty regions.

Three-Loop Sorting

Activity A

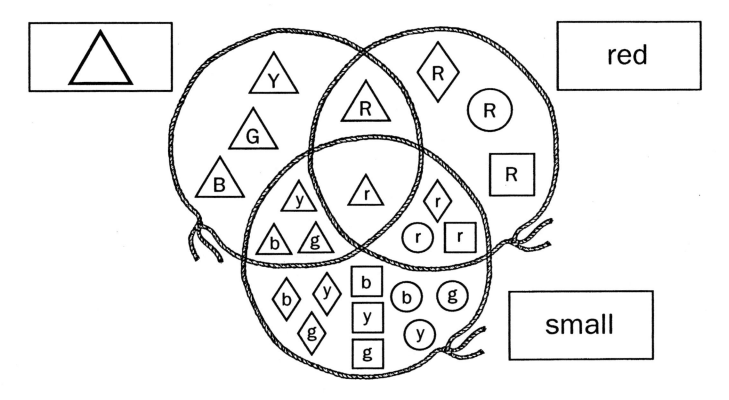

1. How many blocks are both red and small? _____

2. How many blocks are red and small and triangle? _____

3. How many blocks are small? _____

4. How many blocks are red, but not triangle nor small? _____

5. How many blocks are either red or triangle or small? _____

6. How many blocks are either triangle or small? _____

7. How many blocks are in the triangle loop? _____

8. Which blocks are small and triangle, but not red?

Three-Loop Puzzles

Purpose

- To name sets by examining the union and intersection of three sets represented by Venn diagrams

Materials

- ✔ **Three-Loop Puzzles Activity A, B** (pages 81–82), used with 32-block set and label cards
- ✔ **Three-Loop Puzzles Activity C** (page 83), used with 60-block set and label cards
- ✔ Rigid or yarn loops (optional)

Teaching Notes

In **Three-Loop Puzzles**, the students again engage in reverse processing, analyzing the blocks positioned in a three-loop arrangement to identify the sets.

As with the **Two-Loop Puzzles**, some students may find it helpful to recreate the sets pictured on the activity sheets using loops and blocks.

Focus students' attention on the various regions of the arrangement. Ask them to describe the blocks in each region. Some may find it helpful to list this information (on paper or at the board) as they discover it.

Extensions

In the Loops—a game for two players (or two teams).

Use a large piece of paper with three intersecting loops or three overlapping yarn or rigid loops as the playing mat.

- Shuffle the label cards and place them face down in the center of the table.
- The first player selects three label cards, looks at them without showing the other player, and then places them face down, one on each loop.
- The second player chooses a block and tries to locate the region where it belongs. After several blocks have been placed correctly and there are enough clues, the second player tries to identify the sets named on the label cards.
- Players then reverse roles.
- The goal is to identify the three sets with the fewest number of blocks placed.

Three-Loop Puzzles

Activity A

Find the label cards that describe the sets.

1.

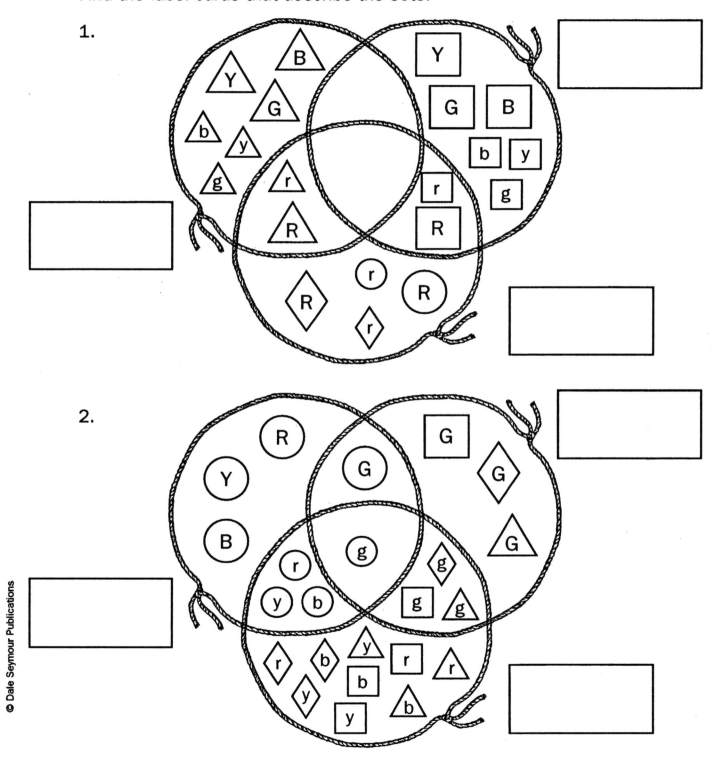

2.

Three-Loop Puzzles

Activity B

Find the label cards that describe the sets.

1.

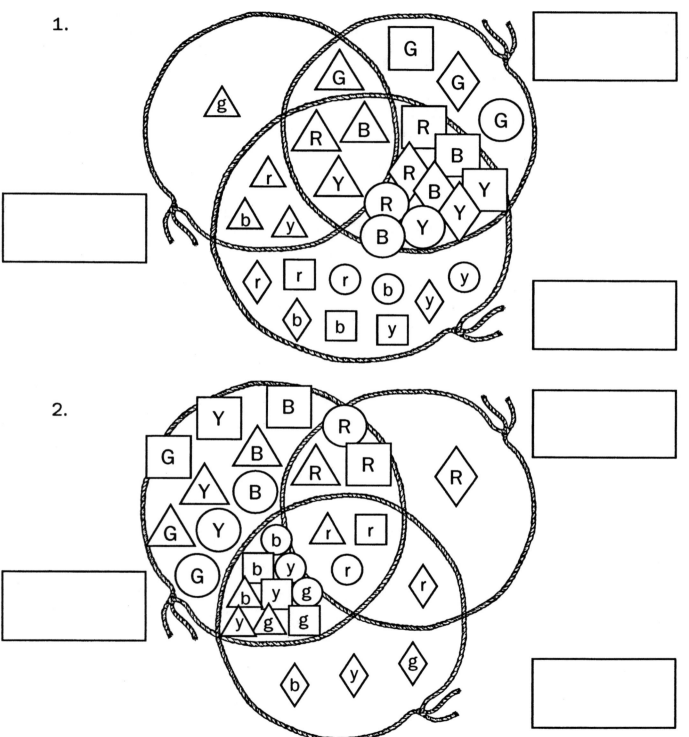

2.

(32-block set)

Three-Loop Puzzles

Activity C

Find the label cards that describe the sets.

1.

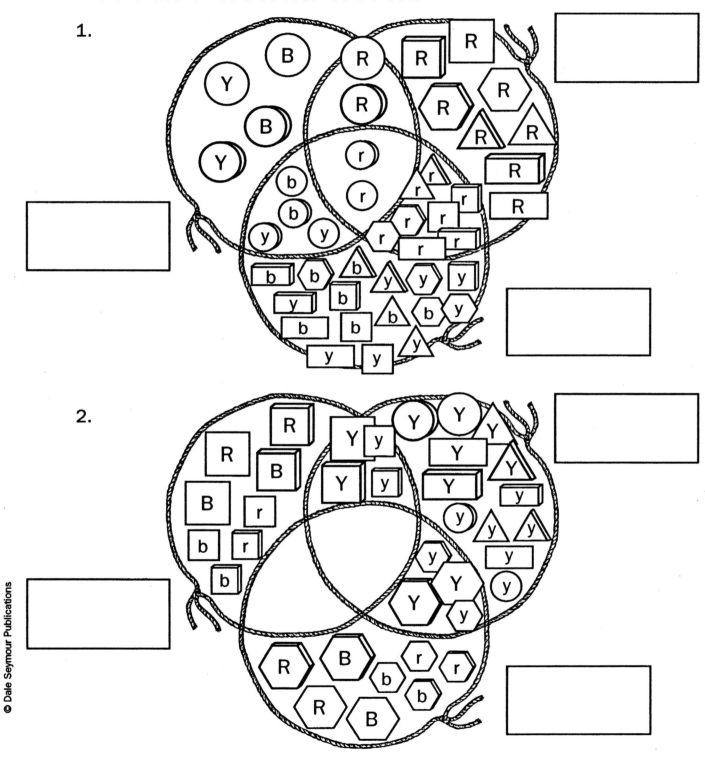

2.

(60-block set)

Three-Loop Mysteries

Purpose

- To examine given overlapping sets represented by Venn diagrams, to correctly label them, and to determine, through logical thinking, which elements are missing.

Materials

✔ **Three-Loop Mysteries Activity A** and **B** (pages 85–86)

✔ **Three-Loop Mysteries Activity C** and **D** (pages 87–88)

✔ 32- or 60-block set, label cards, rigid loops (optional)

Teaching Notes

Three-Loop Mysteries are an extension of the **Two-Loop Mysteries**, presenting three overlapping sets with labels missing and some blocks missing. Students must analyze what is shown, name the sets, and determine which blocks are missing. There is one question mark for each missing block.

As in other activities, allow students to recreate the pictured sets with rigid or yarn loops and the attribute blocks.

The answers to these exercises list first the names of the attributes of the three sets and then the blocks that go with the ?'s. The blocks listed before the first semicolon are those that belong in the top left-hand region of the diagram (A in the diagram below). Those in each regions B–G in the diagram below are listed in alphabetical order with semicolons separating the blocks in each region.

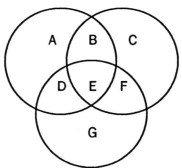

Extensions

Encourage students to create their own **Three Loop Mysteries** using markers or pieces of paper with "?" to represent missing blocks. Before allowing students to exchange puzzles, ask that they explain or demonstrate their solutions to you.

Three-Loop Mysteries

Activity B

Find the missing blocks and the label cards that describe the sets.

1.

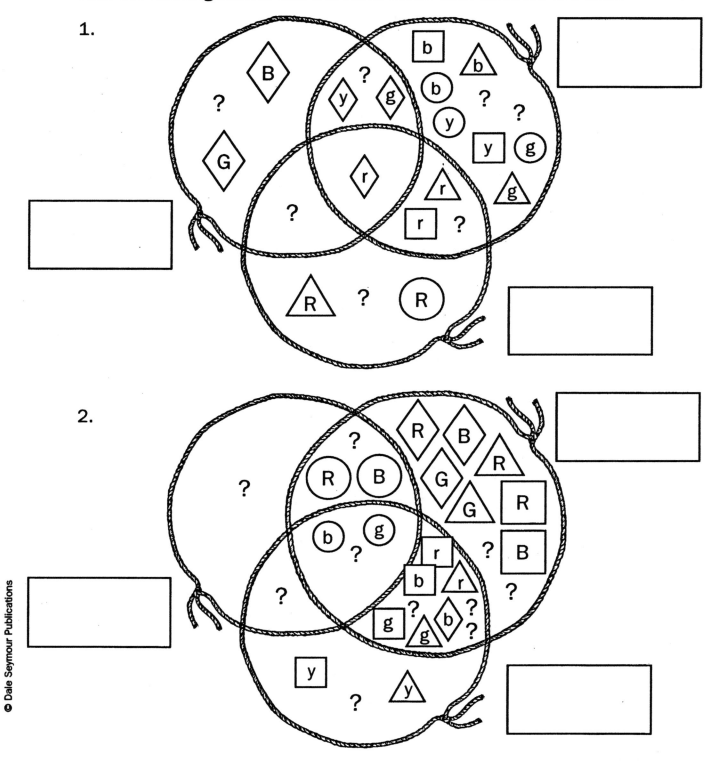

2.

Three-Loop Mysteries

Activity B

Find the missing blocks and the label cards that describe the sets.

1.

2.

(32-block set)

Three-Loop Mysteries

Activity C

Find the missing blocks and the label cards that describe the sets.

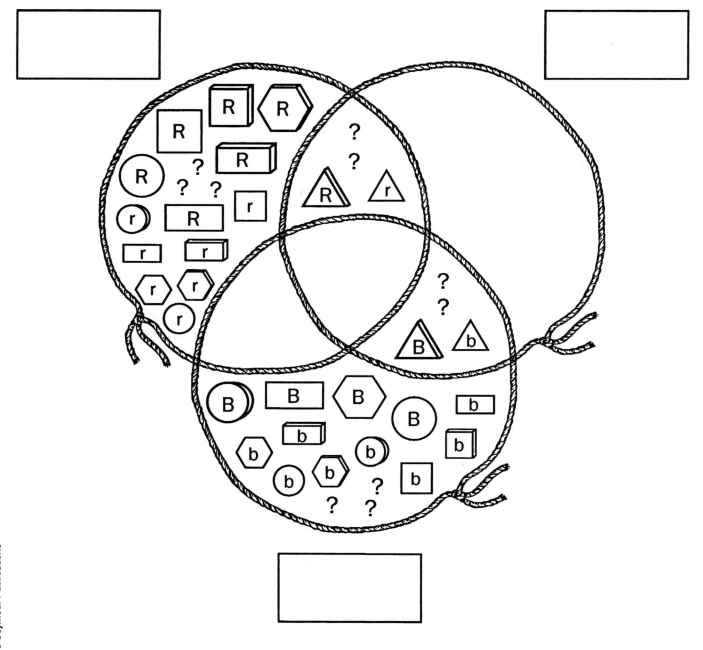

Three-Loop Mysteries

Activity D

Find the missing blocks and the label cards that describe the sets.

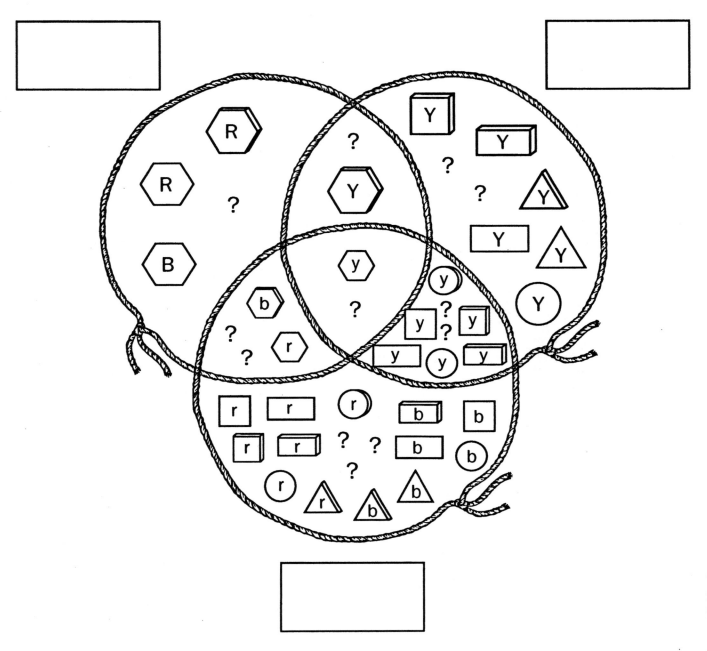

(60-block set)

SECTION

5

Problem Solving

Collecting Data

Purpose

- To gather and display real-world data using a Venn diagram.

Materials

- ✔ Large rigid loops
- ✔ Students' names written on cards
- ✔ Label cards that describe attributes of your students
- ✔ **Collecting Data** (page 91)

Teaching Notes

The activities in Section 5 extend the work with Venn diagrams to a broader problem-solving context. Students discover how they can use Venn diagrams to organize data and to draw conclusions from the data. The emphasis in recording and interpretation is sometimes on the specific elements of a set, other times on the number of elements in a set.

Before beginning the other activities in this section, use data about students in your class. Start with two overlapping loops, one labeled "I have a sister" and the other "I have a brother." Ask students to place their names in one loop, in the space where the loops overlap, or outside the loops. Talk about the number of students that fall into each region.

Ask students to sort themselves according to three different attributes. (The attributes need not be related such as "I walk to school," "I watched the Super Bowl," and "I have a cat.") Ask students to place their names in one of the seven regions of a three-loop Venn diagram. Talk about the number of students whose names are in each region.

Here are other possible labels for your two or three sets.

- I am wearing blue (or red, or tennis shoes, or jeans).

- I watched (name of popular TV show) this week.

- I like apples (or another particular food).

- I have a dog (cat, fish, other pets)

- I would like to visit London (Rome, Cairo, Mexico City)

- I like to read adventures (mysteries, biographies)

Use **Collecting Data** as a worksheet for students to collect data about their classmates. After they have written students' names in one or both of the columns, they can transfer the information to a Venn diagram. Ask students to write about the conclusions they can draw from the data displayed in the Venn diagram.

Collecting Data

Activity A

Survey topics:

A _____

B _____

Record your data.

A	B

Put your data in a two-loop diagram.

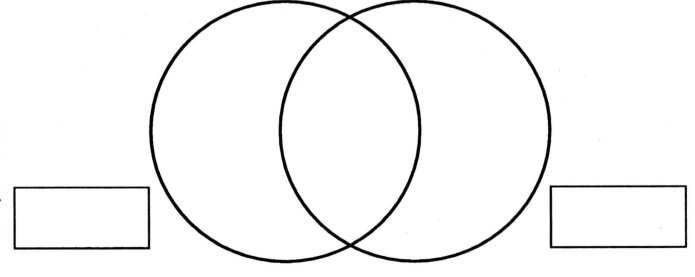

Organizing Data

Purpose

- To organize and display data using a Venn diagram.

Materials

✔ **Organizing Data** (page 93)

Teaching Notes

Organizing Data offers a look at the results of an informal sports survey. Explain that since there are two sets of people involved—the set of people who like basketball and the set of people who like soccer—we can use a two-loop Venn diagram to organize the information. Ask the students to label the two-loop arrangement. Then ask them to identify where each student belongs by writing each name in one region of the Venn diagram.

When the diagrams are complete, ask the following questions:

Who liked both basketball and soccer? (Fernando and Ann)

Who liked basketball? (Sam, Kai, Laura, Ann, and Fernando)

Who liked only soccer? (Michelle, Tom, and Ian)

How many students liked either basketball or soccer? (8)

How many students liked both basketball and soccer? (2)

Organizing Data

A recent survey asked eight people whether they liked basketball or soccer or both. The results of the survey are reported below.

Those who liked basketball:		Those who liked soccer:	
Sam	Ann	Michelle	Fernando
Kai	Fernando	Ann	Ian
Laura		Tom	

Record the names of the students where they belong in the Venn diagram.

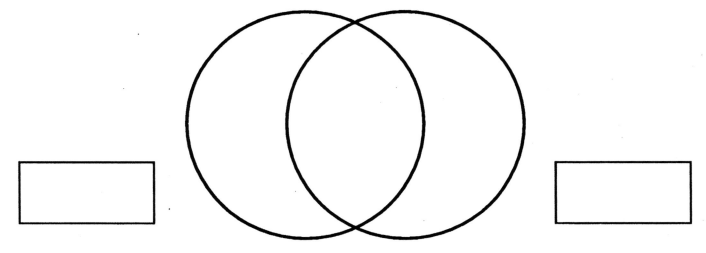

1. Who liked both basketball and soccer?_____

2. Who liked basketball? _____

3. Who liked only soccer? _____

4. How many students liked either basketball or soccer? _____

5. How many students liked both basketball and soccer? _____

Interpreting Data

Purpose

- To read and understand information presented in Venn diagrams.

Materials

✔ **Interpreting Data Activity A, B, C** (pages 95–97)

Teaching Notes

Interpreting Data Activity A shows the data generated from another informal survey involving two sets, with questions that ask students to draw conclusions. **Interpreting Data Activity B** offers a similar survey, this time with data involving three sets.

Be sure to discuss the key connector words *and, or,* and *only* as well as how they apply to the regions of the Venn diagrams. Students are especially likely to be confused by *or*, which, as commonly used, suggests separate and discrete choices—that is, individuals might like either apples or grapes, but not both. They must understand that mathematically, *or* includes the intersection of the two sets—that is, individual who like apples or grapes or *both.*

The data can also be reinterpreted in terms of the number of people in each region of the Venn diagram.

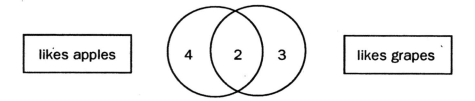

Interpreting Data Activity C shows the results of two surveys in terms of "how many" rather than "who."

Interpreting Data

Activity A

For this survey, people were asked whether they liked apples or grapes or both. Look at the data represented in a Venn diagram and answer the questions.

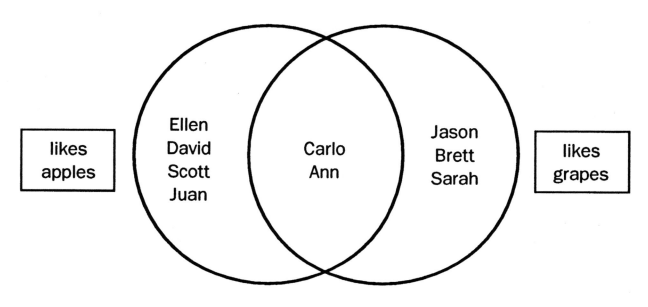

1. Who likes grapes? _____

2. How many people like grapes?_____

3. How many like either apples or grapes, but not both?_____

4. How many like apples and grapes?_____

5. Who likes only apples? _____

6. How many people were there in all?_____

7. State another fact this Venn diagram tells you. _____

_____

Interpreting Data

Activity B

This diagram describes the results of the survey about the winter sports.

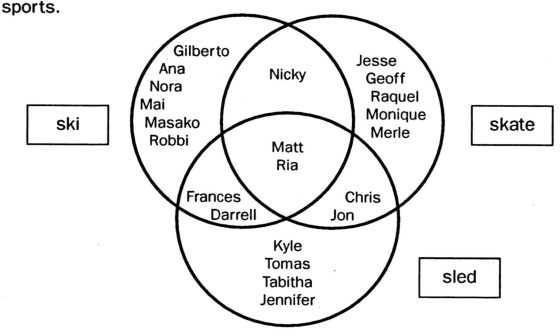

1. How many people were surveyed?_____

2. How many liked either skating or sledding?_____

3. How many people like either skating or skiing?_____

4. Who liked skating and skiing and sledding?_____

5. How many liked only skiing?_____

6. Who liked skiing and sledding, but not skating? _____

7. How many people liked only one sport?_____

8. Who liked skiing and skating? _____

Interpreting Data

Activity C

Exercise Survey:

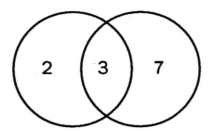

| people who bike | | people who jog |

1. How many people both jog and bike?_____

2. How many people jog?_____

3. How many people either jog or bike?_____

Pet Survey:

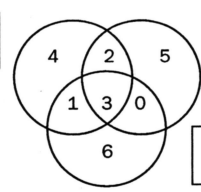

people who have cats as pets

people who have dogs as pets

people who have gerbils as pets

4. How many people have either dogs or cats or gerbils as pets?_____

5. How many people have dogs as pets?_____

6. How many people have either cats or gerbils as pets?_____

7. How many people have only gerbils?_____

Two-Set Problems

Purpose

- To use Venn diagrams as an aid in problem solving and logical thinking.

Materials

✔ **Two-Set Problems Activity A, B, C, D, E , F, G** (pages 99–105)

Teaching Notes

As you introduce the use of Venn diagrams to solve word problems about sets, explain that the focus is on how many people are in each region—not on who is in each set. The students' first task is to identify the specific sets involved.

Use **Two-Set Problems Activity A** to demonstrate how Venn diagrams can help solve problems. Ask four students to read the pieces of information to the class while the other students record the information. Ask students to draw a two-loop Venn diagram, identifying Set A as the people who ate cereal and Set B as the people who ate fruit.

Guide the students as they record the information on the two-loop diagram.

There are 378 who ate cereal, of those, 63 ate fruit also, so 315 (378 – 63) ate only cereal.

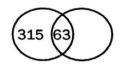

There are 588 people in all, 378 are already accounted for, so 210 (588 – 378) ate only fruit.

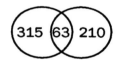

For cooperative groups: **The Two-Set Problems** may be solved cooperatively by four students, each with some information needed to solve the problem. Copy pages 99–105 onto card stock and cut the pieces of information apart. (Cards can be reused by other groups.) Students may read their card to the other members of the group as often as the group asks them to. Together the group will decide what the Venn diagram should look like and what information is needed for each region.

For individual students: Individual students may solve the problems alone using all the information. They can draw the Venn diagrams and write their solutions in their math notebook.

Extensions

Student groups will enjoy devising their own two-set problems and exchanging them with another group.

Two-Set Problems

Activity A

Cereal Survey

A survey found that 588 people ate cereal or fruit for breakfast.

Cereal Survey

Of the people who ate cereal for breakfast, 63 also ate fruit.

Cereal Survey

There were 378 people who ate cereal for breakfast.

Cereal Survey

How many people ate only fruit for breakfast?

Family Survey

In a class of 32 students, 23 of them had a brother or a sister.

Family Survey

Sixteen students have a brother.

Family Survey

Eleven students have a sister. How many students have neither a brother nor a sister?

Family Survey

How many students have both a brother and a sister?

Two-Set Problems

Activity B

Dogs in the Kennel	José and Jonathon own 4 dogs jointly.	**Dogs in the Kennel**	Altogether, José and Jonathon have 12 dogs in their kennel.
Dogs in the Kennel	Jonathon owns 3 dogs himself.	**Dogs in the Kennel**	How many dogs do José and Jonathon each own?

Summer Vacations	Nora has gone on 10 vacations with her parents. Their vacations are always raft trips or hiking.	**Summer Vacations**	On 3 vacations, Nora only went hiking.
Summer Vacations	On 4 vacations, Nora went hiking and on a raft trip.	**Summer Vacations**	How many times did Nora go hiking? How many times did Nora go on a raft trip?

Two-Set Problems

Activity C

Bad Waether	During a particular week, the weather in Seattle was either windy or raining.	Bad Waether	On 4 days, it was raining.
Bad Waether	On 5 days, it was windy.	**Bad Waether**	On some days, it was both windy and raining. How many days was it both?

Dog Food	The dogs at Bingo's Kennel eat either dry kibble or canned dog food. Six of them eat dry kibble.	Dog Food	Six dogs eat only canned dog food.
Dog Food	Two dogs eat both dry kibble and canned dog food.	**Dog Food**	How many dogs are there in Bingo's Kennel?

Two-Set Problems

Frozen Yogurt	In a survey of twelve people, Aaron, Silvia, Paul, and Josh said that their favorite frozen yogurt flavor was raspberry.	**Frozen Yogurt**	Rachel and Danny could not choose, so they said they liked both peach and raspberry.
Frozen Yogurt	Craig, Mark, André, Rita, Barney, and Woody said that their favorite flavor was peach.	**Frozen Yogurt**	How many of the twelve people liked peach?
Favorite Parks	An advertising firm took a survey of 36 twelve-year-olds to find out which was more popular, wild animal parks or amusement parks.	**Favorite Parks**	Sixteen youngsters surveyed said they liked wild animal parks.
Favorite Parks	Twenty-three youngsters surveyed said they liked amusement parks.	**Favorite Parks**	How many of those surveyed liked both wild animal parks and amusement parks?

Two-Set Problems

Activity E

Hot Dogs	At the class picnic, the boys and girls ate 30 hot dogs, all of which were served with either mustard or catsup.	**Hot Dogs**	Five of the hot dogs had both catsup and mustard on them.
Hot Dogs	Twenty of the hot dogs were served with catsup.	**Hot Dogs**	How many people ate hot dogs with some mustard on them?
Gift Wrap Fund Raiser	The school chorus sold gift wrap for their fund-raiser, and 60 people bought something from them.	**Gift Wrap Fund Raiser**	For twenty-six people, curling ribbon was one of the things they ordered.
Gift Wrap Fund Raiser	Twenty-three people bought foil paper but no curling ribbon.	**Gift Wrap Fund Raiser**	Ten people bought both foil paper and curling ribbon. How many bought something other than foil paper or curling ribbon?

Two-Set Problems

Activity F

The results of a survey showed that 64 people get up on the left side of bed all the time.

Some of the 150 people surveyed showed no pattern. That is, they sometimes get up on the left, sometimes the right side of bed.

Fifty-six people said they always get up on the right side of bed.

How many people showed no pattern in how they get out of bed?

A survey showed that 49 middle-school students play soccer or volleyball.

Thirty of the students play volleyball.

Twenty-seven of those students play soccer.

Some of those surveyed play both soccer and volleyball. How many play only soccer?

Two-Set Problems

Activity G

History Test	Ms. Napoleon's history test had two sections. A total of 112 students got A's on at least one part of the test.	**History Test**	On the second section, 90 students got an A.
History Test	On the first section, 42 students got an A.	**History Test**	How many of the students got an A on only one section of the test? How many had A's on both sections?
Basketball Fans	In a particular neighborhood, 20 people cheer for the Boston Celtics.	**Basketball Fans**	Seven people root for both teams.
Basketball Fans	Forty people are fans of the Cleveland Cavaliers.	**Basketball Fans**	If there are 65 people in the neighborhood, how many cheer for neither team?

Three-Set Problems

Purpose

- To use Venn diagrams as an aid in problem solving and logical thinking.

Materials

✔ **Three-Set Problems Activity A, B, C, D, E , F** (pages 107-112)

Teaching Notes

These more challenging activities involve the use of three-loop Venn diagrams in solving word problems about sets. Use **Three-Set Problems Activity A** to lead a class discussion on how to proceed.

Ask students how you should record the problem's information in the diagram to determine the total number of days in all three sets. The suggested procedure is as follows:

- We draw and label the loops—three loops because there are three types of inclement weather.

- It hailed and rained and snowed for 3 days, so we record a 3 in the intersection of the three loops.

- On 4 days it rained and snowed, so we need to show 1 additional day in the snow-rain intersection, making a total of 4 days in the overlapping loops for rain and snow.

- Similarly, it rained and hailed on a total of 5 days, so we conclude that it rained and hailed (but did not snow) on 2 days. Also, since it hailed and snowed on 8 days, it must have hailed and snowed (but not rained) on 5 days.

- We know that it snowed on a total of 13 days. On 9 (1 + 3 + 5 = 9) of those days it also hailed or rained. Therefore, it only snowed on 4 days (13 – 9 = 4). Similarly, we can determine the number of days on which it only hailed (0) or only rained (11).

- To determine the total number of days on which the weather was inclement, we add the number of elements in each region of the diagram: 0 + 5 + 4 + 2 + 3 + 1 + 11 = 26.

Students are to solve the problems on **Three-Set Problems Activity B** through **E** in a similar fashion.

Extensions

Student groups will enjoy devising their own three-set problems and exchanging them with another group.

Three-Set Problems

During the winter vacation, it snowed on 13 days, rained on 17 days, and hailed on 10 days. On 3 days it hailed and rained and snowed. On 4 days it rained and snowed. It rained and hailed on 5 days. It hailed and snowed on 8 days.

Record the information in the three-loop diagram.

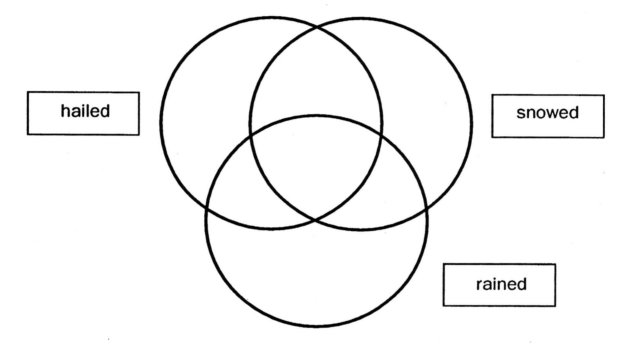

hailed

snowed

rained

On how many days was the weather *inclement:* that is, it either hailed, rained, or snowed?

Three-Set Problems

Activity B

Fifth-grade Survey The students in the fifth-grade classes at King School were surveyed about which school subjects they liked. Eighteen said they liked mathematics.

Fifth-grade Survey Sixteen students liked both English and social studies, but only seven liked both mathematics and English. Nine students liked math and social studies.

Fifth-grade Survey Thirty-two of the students liked English, and twenty-five liked social studies.

Fifth-grade Survey Only three students surveyed said they liked all three subjects. None admitted to disliking all three subjects. How many students were in the fifth grade at King School?

Favorite Music In a survey about popularity of music styles, 200 teenagers were questioned. Twenty-five of those listened to only rap music.

Favorite Music Ten teenagers said they really liked all three styles of music. Seventy teenagers in all liked jazz.

Favorite Music Of the teenagers surveyed, forty liked both rock and jazz. Fifteen listened to both rap and jazz regularly.

Favorite Music In a survey about popularity of music styles among teenagers, twenty-five of those surveyed liked only rock. How many of these teens liked rap music?

Three-Set Problems

Activity C

Teacher's Observations	A math teacher conducted an observation survey of students in her classes. She found that 42 students chewed gum in class, 55 whispered, and 25 fell asleep during class.
Teacher's Observations	Forty students only whispered, and were otherwise cooperative. Ten students whispered and chewed gum, but didn't fall asleep.
Teacher's Observations	Four students whispered and fell asleep, but didn't chew gum. Six students fell asleep and chewed gum, but at least didn't whisper.
Teacher's Observations	There was no student who did not whisper, chew gum, or fall asleep. How many students in all did this teacher have? How many students whispered and chewed gum and fell asleep in class?
Fancy Frog Contest	Ninety people entered the Fancy Frog contest at the Arts & Crafts Festival, creating funny-looking frogs out of clay, wooden sticks, and cotton balls. Forty people used some clay.
Fancy Frog Contest	Twelve people used clay and wooden sticks, but no cotton balls to create their fancy frog. Nine people used cotton balls and clay, but no wooden sticks. Seven used only wooden sticks.
Fancy Frog Contest	Thirteen people used both wooden sticks and cotton balls. Fourteen used only clay.
Fancy Frog Contest	How many people used wooden sticks for the frogs they entered? How many made frogs with all three materials? How many made their frogs with only cotton balls?

Three-Set Problems

Activity D

Flowers for Mother's Day	The seventh-graders surveyed their mothers about what kind of flowers they would most like to get for Mother's Day. Four mothers said they would be equally happy with mums, daisies, and roses.	**Flowers for Mother's Day**	Altogether, thirty mothers would like to get daisies. A total of seventy-five mothers gave their opinions.
Flowers for Mother's Day	Nine mothers said they would like both mums and daisies. How many mothers said they would like mums?	**Flowers for Mother's Day**	Eleven mothers would like to get roses or mums but not daisies. Six said that only mums would do. How many mothers would only like roses for Mother's Day?

Menu Favorites	A group of sixth-graders surveyed their classmates about favorite menus for school lunches. Thirty-two people liked spaghetti. Ten liked both burritos and corn dogs.	**Menu Favorites**	Five of the sixth-graders liked spaghetti and burritos, but not corn dogs. Fourteen liked spaghetti only. How many liked all three menus?
Menu Favorites	Six of the students liked only corn dogs. Seven liked corn dogs and spaghetti, but didn't like burritos.	**Menu Favorites**	Fifty sixth-graders were surveyed; they all liked at least one of the three choices. How many liked burritos but not the other two choices?

Three-Set Problems

Activity E

Motor Club	The local motor club has 45 members. To be a member of the club, a person must drive either a car, a motorcycle, or an all-terrain vehicle. Fourteen members own only cars.	**Motor Club**	One member owns all three—a car, motorcycle, and all-terrain vehicle.
Motor Club	Six members own both a car and a motorcycle. Four members own both a car and an all-terrain vehicle, and two people own a motorcycle and an all-terrain vehicle, but not a car.	**Motor Club**	Ten people own all-terrain vehicles. How many people own motorcycles?
Birthday Wishes	For their birthday each child asked for at least one of the three toys—a bike, video games, or roller blades. Seventeen wanted video games and roller blades. Twelve wanted bikes and roller blades.	**Birthday Wishes**	Five children asked for all three presents. Some children asked for only one item. Sixteen asked for roller blades only.
Birthday Wishes	For their birthday, eight children asked for bikes and video games, but not roller blades.	**Birthday Wishes**	Thirty asked for bikes, and forty-five asked for video games. How many children wanted at least one of the toys?

Three-Set Problems

Activity F

Westside Volunteers — A group calling themselves the Westside Volunteers worked together to fix up a rundown riverside park. Twenty of the volunteers planted trees.	**Westside Volunteers** — Fifteen people helped plant grass and trees. Eight people planted both trees and flowers.
Westside Volunteers — The fifty Westside Volunteers planted trees, flowers, and grass to fix up the park. Thirty people planted flowers, and ten of them planted grass also.	**Westside Volunteers** — Five people worked on all three—trees and flowers and grass. How many people planted grass?

Rusty's Survey — Before having a barbecue, Rusty surveyed his friends to find out which kind of barbecued meat they preferred. He found that 37 people liked steak, 36 liked salmon, and 35 liked chicken.	**Rusty's Survey** — Five people liked steak and chicken, but not salmon. Ten people liked steak only.
Rusty's Survey — Twelve people said they liked salmon and chicken, but didn't like steak. Seven people liked salmon and steak, but not chicken.	**Rusty's Survey** — How many people did Rusty survey? How many people liked all three kinds of barbecued meat?

SECTION

6

Feature Creatures & Hot-Air Balloons

Feature Creatures

Purpose

- To use an alternative set of attribute materials for sorting activities and to extend this attribute set to other attribute activities.

Materials

✔ **Feature Creatures Attribute Set** (page 115) and **Label Cards** (page 116)

✔ **Feature Creatures Activity A, B, C, D, E, F, G** (pages 115–121)

Teaching Notes

There are 54 members of the Feature Creature clan, creatures with four attributes:

HAIR or NO HAIR
Expression: SMILING, FROWNING, PUZZLED
Legs: TWO, THREE, FOUR
Eyes: ONE, TWO, THREE

Copy onto card stock and distribute and ask students to cut into cards **Feature Creatures, Label Cards,** and **Destination Cards** (pages 115–116). Ask students to describe the attributes of these creatures.

   Feature Creatures Activity A, B, C, and **D** are sorting activities. Students use the Feature Creatures and their label cards to determine which Feature Creatures will reach a certain destination or which Feature Creatures have a given preference. Only Feature Creatures with the attribute written on the gate can get past the gate and continue along that path. At each intersection, students must determine which Feature Creatures can continue down each path. **Feature Creatures Activity D** offers an open format map for students to use in making their own map problems. They place label cards on the gates to indicate which Feature Creatures can proceed, and they put destination cards at the ends of the paths. They can use the destination cards provided of invent other destinations.

   Feature Creatures Activity E gives two patterns for students to complete. Students can make their own patterns and arrangements for classmates to complete.

Extensions

You may want to try the Feature Creatures with the following activities:
In the Loop game (page 4), Ten Questions game (page 22), **How Am I Different? Activity C** (page 49), **Difference Trains Activity A** (page 51), **Follow the Arrows Activity C** (page 59), **Different in Both Directions Activity F** (page 66), **Two-Loop Sorting** (page 69)

Feature Creatures

Feature Creatures

Label Cards

smiling	frowning	puzzled	not smiling
not frowning	not puzzled	curly hair	no hair
not curly hair	2 legs	3 legs	4 legs
not 2 legs	not 3 legs	not 4 legs	1 eye
not 1 eye	2 eyes	not 2 eyes	3 eyes
not 3 eyes			

Destination Cards

swimming	walking	video games	soccer
volleyball	reading	biking	

comedy	adventure	science fiction	classic
cartoon	musical	drama	oldie

Feature Creatures

Activity A

Getting to Town

The Feature Creatures must pass through the gate to get to town.
Only those with a puzzled expression can pass.

How many Feature Creatures get to town? _____

Which ones get past the gate? _____

Going to the Movies

To get the movies, the Feature Creatures must get past two gates.
Only those with hair can get past the first gate and only those with
two legs can get past the second gate.

How many Feature Creatures get to see the movie? _____

Which Feature Creatures get to the movies? _____

Feature Creatures

Activity B

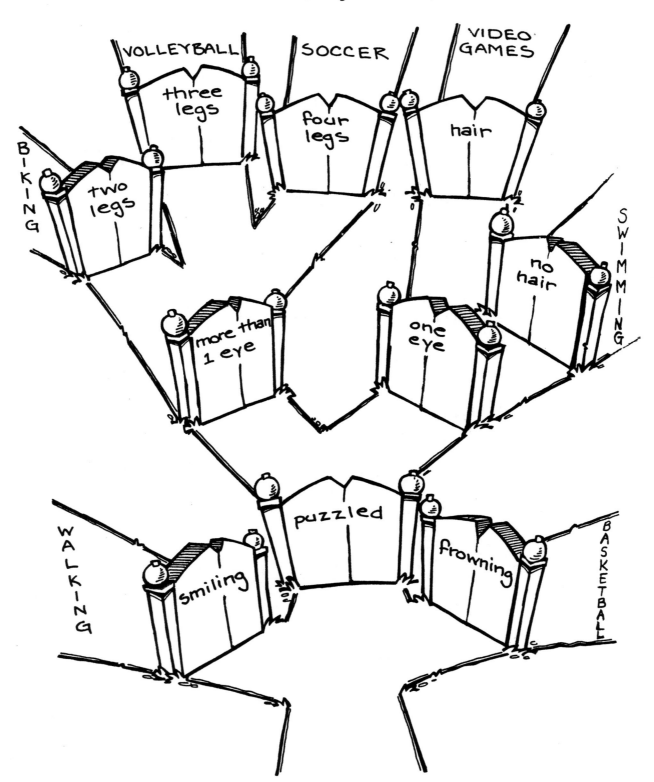

Feature Creatures

Activity C

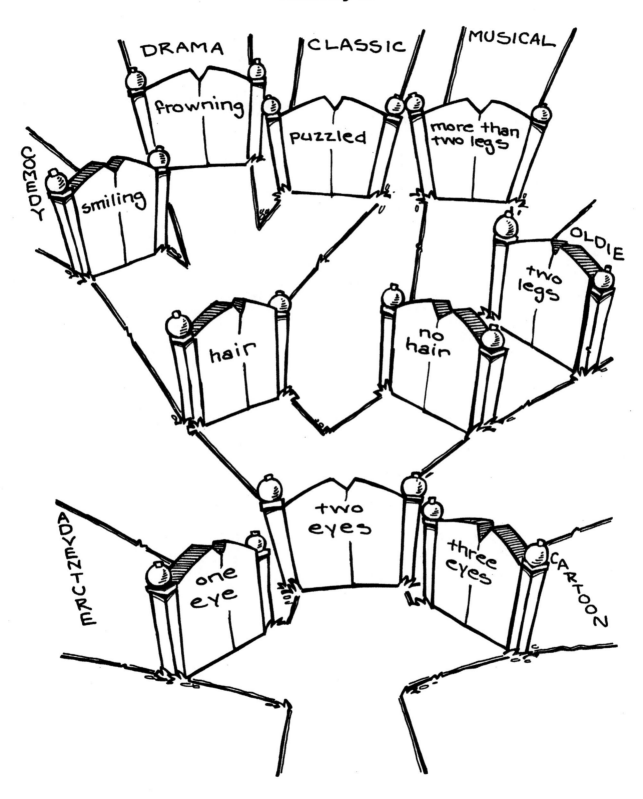

Feature Creatures

Activity D

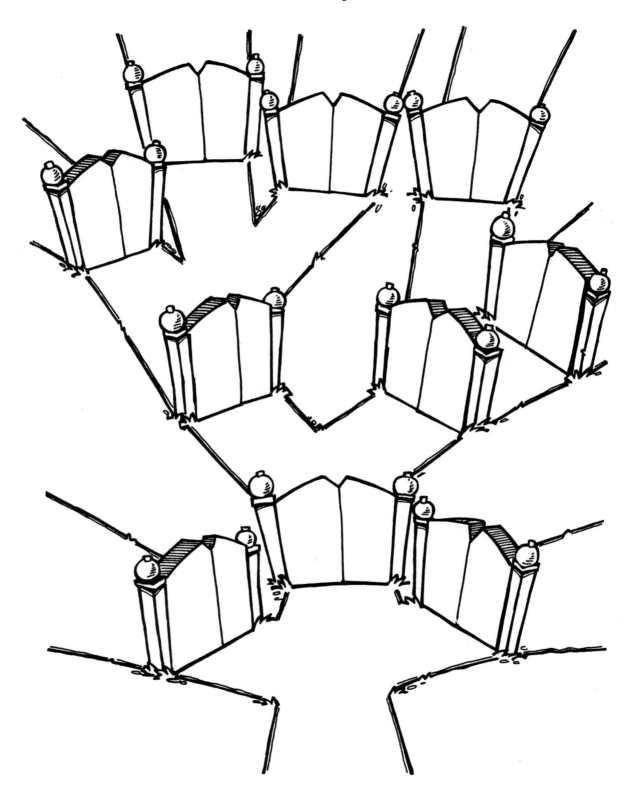

Feature Creatures

Activity E

What is missing in these patterns? Continue the patterns.

1.

?

?

2.

?

?

?

Hot-Air Balloons

Purpose

- To use an alternative set of attribute materials to extend problem solving to other attribute activities.
- For older students: To understand the relationship between the number of blocks in an attribute set and the number of values each attribute has.

Materials

✔ **Hot-Air Balloons** (page 123)—three copies on card stock to make each set of attribute cards

✔ **Hot-Air Balloons Activity A, B, C** (pages 124–126)

Teaching Notes

Students can make their own 27-piece attribute set by coloring each of three pages of balloons in a different color or a different color combination; each page must be colored consistently in one color scheme and the colors must be distinct from page to page (red, blue, and yellow are named on the activity sheets). Cut the cards apart after they are colored.

On **Hot-Air Balloons Activity A, B, C,** the students must identify several missing blocks in an array of rows and columns, just as they did for the **Complete the Arrangement** activities. Because this set has three values for each of three attributes (size: large, medium, small; balloon pattern: stripes, star, dots; and color) many arrangements in 3-by-3 arrays can be made. Since each attribute has the same number of values, any attribute can change across the rows or down the columns. After solving **Hot-Air Balloons Activity A, B, C,** students can use the hot-air balloon attribute cards to create their own arrays of balloons.

Values of Attributes. With older students, you might introduce the concept of the values of an attribute. In the 32-block set, the attribute of color has 4 values (red, green, yellow, and blue); the attribute of size has 2 values (large and small); and the attribute of shape has 4 values (square, circle, diamond, circle). Therefore, there are 4 x 2 x 4 = 32 attribute blocks in the set. Suppose we designed a set of attribute blocks that had 5 attributes. Let's say that the first attribute had 3 values; the second, 3 values; the third, 4 values; the fourth, 2 values; the fifth, 3 values. How many blocks would be in the complete set? (3 x 3 x 4 x 2 x 3 = 216)

Extensions

This set of attribute cards can also be used with other activities in this book, such as those listed for the **Feature Creatures** on page 114.

Hot-Air Balloons

Pattern for a 27-piece attribute set

Make three copies—color each copy a different color.

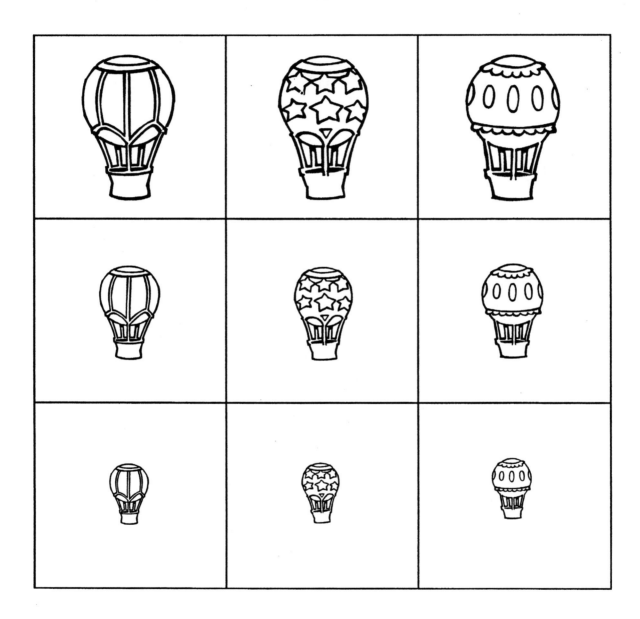

ot-Air Balloons

Activity A

Complete the arrangement.

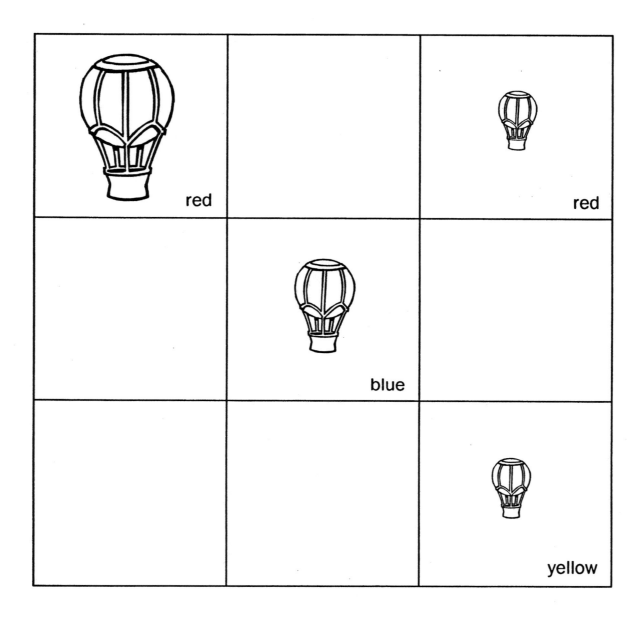

Hot-Air Balloons

Activity B

Complete the arrangement.

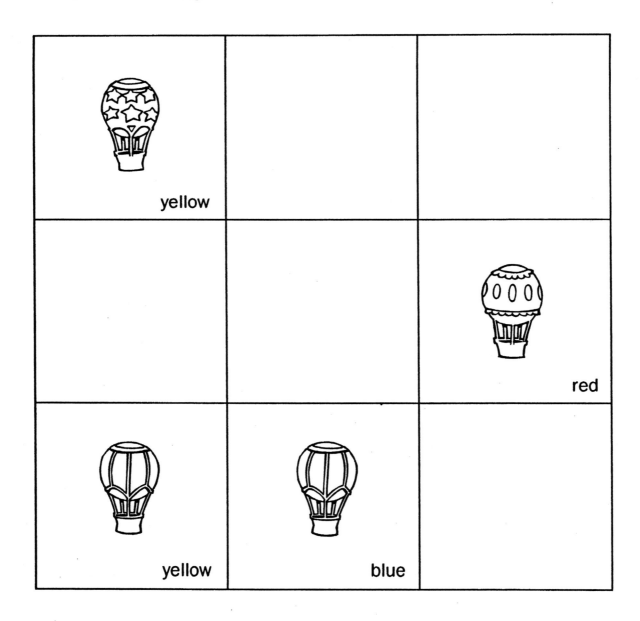

Hot-Air Balloons

Activity C

Complete the arrangement.

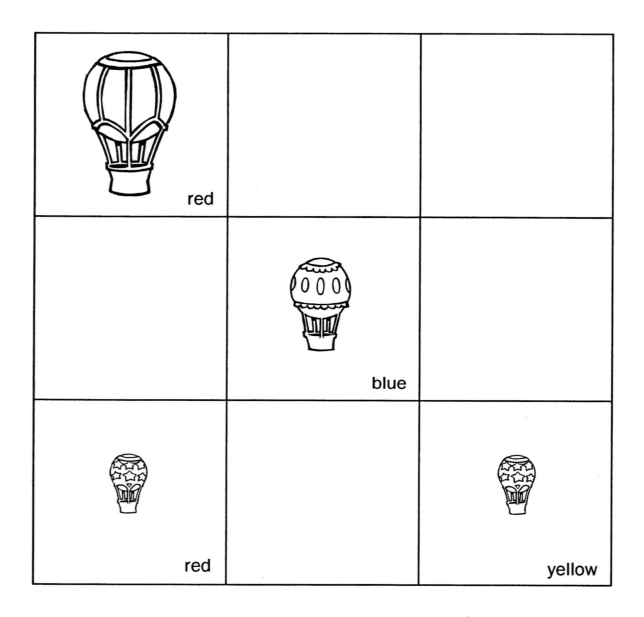

Solutions

Page 3 **(32-block set)** The sets that can be described by one attribute are: 4 color sets: red, green, yellow, blue; 4 shape sets: square, circle, triangle, diamond; 2 size sets: large, small. **(60-block set)** The sets that can be described by one attribute are: 3 color sets: red, blue, yellow; 5 shape sets: square, circle, triangle, rectangle, hexagon; 2 size sets: large, small; 2 thickness sets: thick, thin.

Page 5 **(32-block set)** 8 triangles, 24 outside   **(60-block set)** 12 triangles, 48 outside

Page 6 **(32-block set)** 8 red blocks, 24 outside   **(60-block set)** 20 red blocks, 40 outside

Page 7 answers will vary

Page 9 **1.** small **2.** circle **3.** red

Page 10 **1.** triangle **2.** large **3.** diamond

Page 11 **1.** blue **2.** square **3.** yellow

Page 12 **1.** green **2.** not-triangle **3.** not-red

Page 13 **1.** hexagon **2.** yellow **3.** thick

Page 14 **1.** triangle **2.** large **3.** blue

Page 15 **1.** rectangle **2.** square **3.** red

Page 16 **1.** thin **2.** circle **3.** small

Page 17 **1.** not-hexagon **2.** not-red

Page 19 **1.** *attribute:* triangles; *?'s:* large yellow triangle, large blue triangle, small red triangle **2.** *attribute:* red; *?'s:* large red diamond, small red triangle

Page 20 **1.** *attribute:* small; *?'s:* small red circle, small blue square, small yellow diamond, small green diamond, small green circle **2.** *attribute:* diamonds; *?'s:* large green diamond, large red diamond, small blue diamond, small yellow diamond

Page 21 **1.** *attribute:* red; *?'s:* thick large red circle, thin large red square, thin large red hexagon, thick small red rectangle, thick small red triangle, thin small red rectangle **2.** *attribute:* hexagon; *?'s:* thin large red hexagon, thick large blue hexagon, thin small red hexagon, thin small yellow hexagon, thick large yellow hexagon

Page 23 **(32-block set) 1.** 4 color sets **2.** 8 blocks each **3.** 4 shape sets **4.** 8 blocks each **5.** 2 size sets **6.** 16 blocks each **7.** 32 **8.** 24 **9.** 4 **10.** 6 **11.** 4 **12.** 12 **(60-block set) 1.** 3 color sets **2.** 20 blocks each **3.** 5 shape sets **4.** 12 blocks each **5.** 2 size sets **6.** 30 blocks each **7.** 60 **8.** 48 **9.** 10 **10.** 8 **11.** 6 **12.** 24

Page 24 **1.** 8 **2.** 24 **3. and 4.** large or small **5.** any shape set or any color set **6.** large blocks of any shape or color or small blocks of any shape or color **7.** not color or not shape **8.** large (or small) not shape (or not color) **9.** The block must have 3 attributes (e.g. large red triangle)

Page 25 **1.** 12 **2.** 40 **3 and 4.** large (or small) or thick (or thin) **5.** not color **6.** thick (or thin) large (or small) any color **7.** must have 4 attributes **8.** not shape **9.** thick (or thin) not shape or large (or small) not shape **10.** large (or small) and thick (or thin)

Page 27 **1.** small red square **2.** small green circle **3.** small blue triangle **4.** large yellow diamond **5.** large red triangle **6.** answers will vary

Page 28 **1.** small thick yellow rectangle **2.** large thin red hexagon **3.** small thin blue circle **4.** large thick blue square **5.** large thick red hexagon **6.** answers will vary

Page 31 **1.** small yellow square, large green square (or large red not square) *rule:* keep shape constant for 8 (or 6 blocks); alternate large and small; two red, two blue, two yellow **2.** small yellow diamond, small blue diamond, large red circle (or large red triangle) *rule:* four large shapes (first two the same and last two the same), four small shapes (first two the same and last two the same); red, green, yellow, blue

Page 32 **1.** large green diamond, small yellow triangle, small red square *rule:* red, green, yellow; 2 small, 2 large; triangle, square, circle, diamond **2.** large red diamond, large yellow triangle, small yellow circle *rule:* red, yellow, yellow, red, yellow, yellow; 4 small, 4 large; circle, square, diamond, triangle

Page 33 **1.** small red square, large green (or other not red) circle *rule:* large, small; circle, triangle, square; 6 red, 6 another color **2.** small red triangle, large red triangle, small blue diamond (or rectangle or square or hexagon) *rule:* four triangles, four circles, four of another shape; 2 blue, 2 red; small, large, small, large

Page 34 **1.** large thick red circle, large thin red rectangle (or hexagon) *rule:* thin, thick; large; 6 (or 8 or 10) red; 2 squares, 2 triangles, 2 circles, (repeat with different color or follow by two red rectangles) **2.** large thin yellow triangle, large thick red circle (or rectangle) *rule:* thick, thin; large; red, blue, yellow; 2 of one shape followed by 2 of a different shape

Page 35 **1.** thin small red hexagon, thick large blue rectangle (or triangle), thick small red rectangle (or triangle) *rule:* thick, thin; blue, red; large, small, small; two of one shape, then two of a different shape **2.** large thin red rectangle, small thin yellow square, large thin blue triangle, *rule:* blue, yellow, red, yellow; alternate large, small; circle, rectangle, square, triangle, hexagon

Page 37 rows maintain color (yellow, blue, red, green); columns maintain shape (square, triangle, circle, diamond); they are all large

Page 38 rows maintain shape and alternate large/small (large circle, small circle, large triangle, small triangle); columns maintain color (red, blue, yellow, green)

Page 39 rows maintain shape and alternate small/large; the first two columns are blue and the last two columns are green

Page 40 rows maintain color and rows 1–3 consist of thin blocks, rows 4–6 consist of thick blocks; columns maintain shape (square, triangle, rectangle, circle, hexagon)

Page 41 rows maintain shape; columns maintain size and thickness (thin small, thin large; thick small, thick large)